CAMP 38

by
Jill von Konen

Published by
SOVEREIGN PRESS
326 Harris Road
Rochester, WA 98579

ISBN 0-914752-19-7

Library of Congress Catalog Card Number 83-51819

Manufactured in the United States of America

To

John, and all the people

at the real Camp 38

"How beauteous is mankind,

O brave new world that has

such people in it."

STATEMENT OF THE KNOWN FACTS

In San Francisco, last April, a man in his early twenties was hit by a city bus on Van Ness Avenue and died before reaching the hospital. There were many witnesses and the investigation was routine; the death was officially recorded as accidental. The victim aroused some interest because the lack of identification was so complete it looked purposeful. He had a new billfold with over eight hundred dollars but no identifying cards, no cleaning or laundry marks on his clothes, and there was no record of his fingerprints.

I am a reporter for the San Francisco Post-Intelligencer. When the accident occurred I chanced to be driving behind the bus. A patrol car was also in the block; the police and I reach the accident at the same time and, while we were crawling under the bus to get to the already unconscious man, I found a red book on the street about four feet from the victim. Thinking it might be an angle on the story, I started to put it in my purse until I had time to look at it. One of the officers saw what I was doing and insisted on taking it from me. I let him have it at the time but, as the connection with the deceased had not been established, I later filed a claim to it as its finder. On the book were no traces of the victim's fingerprints, but they could easily have been destroyed by mine or those of the police officer, and I am frankly of the opinion that the book was on the young man's person at the time of the accident. However, because there was no conclusive evidence to that effect, a quirk of law makes it mine. It is now in my possession.

It is a red cloth bound diary, six by nine inches in size, with full pages for each day of the year. The front pages up to January twenty-one had been torn out and the book then reused without regard to printed dates. The context of the diary makes it clear that if dates had been used they would not have been those of our calendar.

At the time I found the book a folded letter in an unsealed, unaddressed envelope was closed within its pages. A photograph of the letter showing the handwriting, and a photograph of the diary were part of my story on the accident which appeared on page one of my paper.

For reasons that are obvious from their contents, both the letter and the diary appear intended for personal delivery by the accident victim as a precaution against their falling into the wrong hands. An additional reason — that of introducing the young man to the girl to whom the letter was addressed — appears a high probablilty. Both letter and diary are reprinted here in full without editing. Only one thing has been added. The separate, undated entries in the diary have been numbered consecutively like chapters in a book.

Dear Peg,

Your moment for a big decision has arrived. You are to decide whether you want to join me here but I can't tell you where I am. My diary will give you some idea of what my life is like but even that you can't have to mull over at leisure. You can read it only when you're with Douglas, who's bringing it to you. He won't leave it with you even for a short while for fear someone else might see it and become curious.

You've probably wondered why I couldn't tell you where I was going when I left with Kirk. If you come, Douglas will bring you and you'll have to trust him completely, as I trusted Kirk. You will not know where you're going.

I've often thought of you since that night we said a quick goodby in the hallway, and wished I could see you. I think you'd be happier here and I'd like terribly to see you but I don't want to persuade you. It should be entirely your choice. Think it over carefully — it has to be a one time decision — no turning back. If you don't come you'll probably never see me or hear from me again but, whatever you decide, you may be sure that you'll always have my love.

Valerie

DIARY

1.

I have an impulse to write but it seems crazy. I'm no more trying to communicate with anyone than a new born baby is when it lets out its first cry.

Birth. A broken cord, and a scream at the first moment of freedom.

Traumatic individuation. No scream. I just pick up a pen and start scribbling.

The baby's cry is instinctive and serves to fill its lungs with air. Mine is a learned behavior. Because I'm a product of sixteen years schooling, I've succumbed to the peculiar civilized practice of turning big healthy screams into neat rows of little words. But is my learned behavior even as effective as the baby's instinct? Will undirected writing bring a breath of freshness from the whole world to ventilate my being and give life to my psyche?

Maybe I'm less than the baby. I might be more like a conditioned computer. But I can't believe a computer feels. I feel. My aloneness hurts like a great gnawing emptiness in the pit of my stomach.

This loneliness is strange. My emotions surprise me. I'm here voluntarily; I'm with the man I love; there are English speaking people all around me, but I'm alone in a way I never before imagined — the tie with my past has been broken. I knew that was going to happen and didn't think it would be important. But an unexpected, odd sort of aloneness connected with it has come upon me like a catastrophic external force.

Kirk had some idea of what it would be. He warned me. He studied me carefully, wanting to be sure I could take it.

He gave me sleeping pills to keep me from knowing where I am and how we got here. I could also think of them as an anesthetic for an operation to individuate me, except that the break in time and place while I was knocked out is a big part of the thing that affects me. The suddenness and completeness of the change is what gets me. During the time I was doped, the umbilical cord (to use the hackneyed idea again) was cut and all traces of it removed. It's left me completely disoriented.

I feel sure I wasn't knocked out more than two days. No real evidence: it's just the way my body feels. If that's right we can't very well be more than a thousand miles from San Francisco. Not unless we switched to a plane. Kirk gave me two capsules of something. I took them with coffee and went to sleep in the back of the station wagon.

When I woke up we were at an isolated cabin in the woods and there was no trace of the car. Instead of the car there were two horses, just standing in a little corral as if someone had brought them and taken the car away. We made the last half day's trip here on horseback. I have a hunch we went all the way from the place we were parked at the Marina Yacht Harbor in San Francisco to that first cabin in the woods with me asleep in the back of the station wagon.

I can't believe we switched to a plane. Somehow I feel that Kirk wouldn't have subjected me to a conspiracy where he had to depend on others to help in moving my unconscious body. When he offered me those pills and asked me to take them, I felt that I was trusting myself blindly to him and him alone. I still felt so when I woke up in the cabin at the beginning of the horse trail here — hours or days later. I still trust him completely.

It's finding myself among others — others like Kirk but unlike me — that brings on my sense of aloneness. I hadn't really known that he was as different from me as he is until I saw him among his own kind. Either they don't know it exists or they deliberately avoid any reference to the world I have always known. I suppose I shouldn't consider the possibility that they don't know. They have to know; I knew Kirk in that other world. He has gone back and forth between the two. He knows, so the others who accept him must know. But no one will talk of it to me.

Last night at the party — a party in my honor — I tried a dozen times to get someone to acknowledge the existence of things that have always been familiar to me — California, San Francisco, the United States, China, Russia, Germany — and always the same casual "I don't relate to San Francisco," "I don't relate to the United States," "I don't relate to Russia," "No, I also don't relate to the Soviet Union."

8

At last, in exasperation, I asked one highly intelligent and kindly old man, "Well, what *is* beyond this valley, beyond the surrounding forests, beyond the places and people to whom you do relate?"

"There is a big area overrun by zombis, the world as you have known it."

"And am *I* a zombi?" I pressed him — more than a little belligerently I'm sure.

He looked deep in my eyes, smiled, and, without the slightest displacement of poise, said, "You seem to be awakening quite well."

And that's the way it is. I made a pact with Kirk that I wouldn't ask *him* where we were for a full month before he would bring me here — wherever here is — and no one else here "relates" to the world outside. I know now how it would feel to wake up in an insane asylum after a severe psychosis. One would try to talk of the private world from which he was emerging — a world that might have seemed much more real than reality — and everyone would say, "That, my dear girl, was a fantasy of yours. You must understand that I can't know it."

And the patient would say, "I'll tell you about it."

"No. It would be better if you wouldn't dwell on it. You need to rebuild your bridge to reality."

That's precisely the attitude of the kind, intelligent, old man who said to me, "You seem to be awakening quite well." He was a scholarly sort with white hair and grey eyes. He was an old man but his eyes weren't old; they were still intensely interested in life. I liked him a lot. He didn't strike me as being the mad scientist type. I thought of him as possibly a professor in the humanitites. Certainly I didn't think he would do anything to hurt me. But I don't know what to think about his attitude. It is almost impossible to believe this world and the attitude of these people is real and I know the world *I came from is real.* I was born in San Francisco and have lived there all my twenty-one years. I got my degree in anthropology from U.C. Berkeley last spring. Before then my world might have had a little bit of schoolgirl vagueness in it, but it became real in a hurry. I had always made jokes about what I was going to do when I got my degree but didn't really believe it. Then I did exactly that. I got a typing job in a freight office and started dating a truck driver.

I thought Kirk Morgan was an *unusual* truck driver. Not just unusually good looking, though he was that, too, but unusual in some strange, mysterious, undefinable way. It was so completely the way I had joked about it that I tried to keep my feelings about his unusualness to myself. After knowing him only a few weeks — and actually knowing absolutely nothing about him — I agreed to go away with him to an unknown destination without telling anyone.

That was a crazy thing to do, maybe, but I am real, Kirk is real, and the people here are real. Only this refusal to accept the world I have known makes no sense to me. I vaguely suspect it may have a purpose, maybe an exceptionally good purpose. It's intensifying my awareness of things; it's "awakening" me. I don't think it was designed for my benefit but maybe it does something like that to everybody. Anyway it seems all right. I can accept it because Kirk is here and the people here are the nicest I have ever met.

But the break with the past, the sense of being cut adrift with no orientation except "I am I, here is here, and now is now" is an unexpectedly wierd experience.

Last night in a big rough-hewn hall, a place with a sort of old Viking grandeur, I met, laughed, ate, and danced with maybe fifty men, women, and children. Then Kirk and I came back here where we had aleready been alone for two days. I am alone now in the afternoon and he has gone to some unspecified place with the promise that he would be back by sunset. We are living in a stone and log cabin all by itself out in the woods. It is simple but good, well built and in good taste. There is plenty of food. The food is all in permanent stainless steel, glass, and ceramic containers — not the disposable tin cans I have always known. Except for little things like that nothing is unusual and I have done nothing unusual. Right now I am planning to make dinner in expectation of Kirk's return and set a handmade, antuqie looking table that is in one end of the living room. There is a big fireplace, some blue earthen dishes that I fell in love with at first sight, and a hand loomed table cloth of varicolored threads that harmonizes with the dishes. I will pick some flowers for the table and everything will be beautiful.

This is reality and it is good. But I am disturbed by my inability to "relate" to my past, to San Francisco and to my sister, Peg, who I am sure still lives, at this very moment, in an apartment on Leavenworth Street we both shared there — wherever there is in relation to here.

Everything is wonderful except that the situation makes no

sense to me. To be faced with the question of who and what one is when one's past "does not relate" is an amazingly complex nothingness. I had better forget it and go pick the flowers.

2.

The refusal of the people here to talk about the outside world may be primarily a policy in child training. Today I took a long walk in the woods and met a group of children whose training seemed radically different from that of other children I've known. I saw seven ranging from about five to about thirteen years old and I sensed that there were several others who didn't show themselves. They were playing a game that I suppose might be called "settlement expedition." They were pretending to be settling a new land. Some were too young to have acquired disciplined reserve but even the older ones talked quite openly and frankly with me. I'm very fond of children and get along well with them. I joined them in their game for two or three hours and became well acquainted. I'm sure they know absolutely nothing of the world beyond these forests. And they are *not* curious. That lack of curiosity has to be the result of carefully oriented training. They are obviously convinced that the "outside" world has nothing in it that they want.

When I found that they were pretending to be settling a new land I mentioned the Pilgrims and the Plymouth Rock settlement.

"I don't understand you," a little boy of about eleven said. "That must be zombi language."

Most of them stopped in their construction of a cave-house when I came up. They seemed happy to see me and talk to me. I didn't surprise them. Part of their game was to have lookouts in all directions and word of my approach had been passed on ahead of me.

"What do you know about zombis and zombi language?" I asked.

"We know you came from zombiland only five days ago," a little girl about seven piped up. "Don't you remember me?" she added. "I met you at the party three nights ago."

"Oh, yes. Of course I remember you." I held out my arms to her. Instead of giving herself into my arms she merely took both my hands in both of hers. She smiled and seemed sincerely glad to see me but showed a reserve that seemed a little too mature for her.

"I'm glad you remember me," she added. "I like you. I feel

11

that almost everyone will be glad you have come."

I wondered how I could have forgotten her. She was a strikingly beautiful little girl with extremely proud bearing and dark eyes and dark hair. She must have been at least half American Indian. I suddenly realized that she did not stand out in my memory because I had been so overwhelmed at the party by her sort that the striking had become commonplace — happy, intelligent eyes, beautiful skin coloring, good features, and well shaped heads carried with regal pride. At least a fourth of the people I have met here are predominately American Indian or Oriental heritage. I am reasonably sure that people of American Indian, Chinese, and Japanese blood are here, along with European races. Also there may be some people here from the Pacific Islands but I'm not sure. The mixing seems to be only a few generations back and some are obivously all Oriental or American Indian and some are all Northern European. The children were a fair sampling of the people who had been at the party. I looked them all over quickly but could remember seeing none at the party but the girl. I hope I didn't give the impression of being too much of a zombi by failing to recognize some of the others.

"Where is this zombiland you talk of and what do you think it is like?" I asked and looked around at the six children who had stopped their work to talk to me (one boy had continued working after a brief glance in my direction). No one answered. They seemed to ponder the question.

Finally a very small boy with blue eyes and curly blond hair asked, "Don't you know where you came from?"

"I know," I said (and wondered if I really did). "But do you know? Where is zombiland and how would you describe a zombi?"

He didn't seem to be able to answer. After a minute the oldest boy in the group stepped forward. He was about thirteen. Apparently he was the leader, although the game seemed so familiar that it required no overt leadership. Anyway he took it upon himself to give me a straight answer. I decided afterwards that it was not done to show off his knowledge but because he felt it the kind thing to do.

"We call most of the world zombiland because it is overrun by zombis," he said. "There are a few settlements like Camp 38 but on a world map they are so small that they just look like dots. Zombis are people who have become sort of sleep walkers. They speak and understand a language that doesn't relate to reality, and their actions can be completely controlled through this language. Some

12

zombis have been given names or titles which makes the others think of them as controllers; when they use words in a certain way all the other zombis do what they are told."

"Like magic?" I asked. I thought I understood him but it seemed a strangely erudite comment on the world to be coming from a boy still playing children's games, so I wanted to be sure. I pretended not to understand so as to make him refute me.

"No. There's nothing undiscoverable in the way the words are used to control zombi actions. It's just complex and requires much attention."

"Do you know enough of the zombi language to give me an example of the way zombis control zombis?"

"No. I've heard some examples but the concepts behind the words zombis use are very confused and so they are hard to remember. I don't recall the sounds of the words either. They have a word — nation, I think it is — that is used to designate a fictitious entity. The same unreal entity is called fatherland or motherland to suggest to the confused mind that it should be looked upon as a parent. Then certain controller-zombis are given certain things that they can say which will be heard by the others as if it were the voice of the imaginary entity — the fatherland or whatever it is. In that way a non-existent parent is believed to be speaking and adults obey as if they were little children."

"You seem to know more than you take credit for. Would you like me to tell you more about zombis and zombiland?"

"No. I understand that it would be a fatal strategy to try colonizing zombiland by relating to zombi concepts. The people colonizing would become zombis. And just to study it for idle amusement or in the hope of salvaging some of the fully conditioned zombis I think would be a poor use of my time and effort. I would not want to become seriously interested in psychiatry."

The word "psychiatry" hit me full in the face. I remembered what I was writing a couple of days ago, comparing my feelings to the awakening of a patient in an insane asylum, and thought it was time to demonstrate my sanity. I asked about what they were building. They showed me readily and accepted me into their game as if I were just another child come out to play with them.

It was not the usual feeling I have as an adult playing with children. Their construction showed advanced skill. They were as good or better at what they were doing than I was and there didn't seem to be the usual rigid line drawn between children and adults. During the day I picked up a lot of stray bits of attitudes. I may

13

try to put some of them down later but I want to stop writing and take another walk now.

3.

There was a big noise in the woods a few minutes ago, something crashing through the brush. I thought it might be a bear. Although I had already looked the house over carefully a dozen times, I went all over it again, this time hunting for any possible hiding place for a rifle. I didn't find one. I finally went out empty handed to look around, I could see nothing. I suppose it was some animal — bear or deer. We certainly are not overrun by people here.

I have been alone for two days. Except for Kirk at night and the children yesterday I have seen no one.

Today I have been going over in my mind the attitudes of those children. More than anything else and more than most children — or maybe just more conspicuously — they seem to fear social ostracism. I have no idea what sort of government keeps order here but I have been wondering if there could possibly be criminal courts that handed down no other penalty than ostracism. It seems impractical. But the idea that it might be true got hold of me. That repeated phrase, "I don't relate," kept coming back to my mind. Alone here in the woods, waiting for Kirk to return from an unknown place, I have become almost terrified at the thought that people might decide not to relate to me.

Absolute freedom suddenly seems much more horrible than "the pressures of society." Suppose Kirk never came back. Suppose no children welcomed me happily into their games. Suppose I took a long walk and managed to find the hall where we had the party in my honor the other night, and found that all those wonderful people refused "to relate" to me. Suppose I wandered on through the woods to new communities and new cities and no one would acknowledge my existence. I would do some small criminal act to prod people into noticing me and giving me attention — even unkind attention — and no one would do more than walk around me as if I were an inanimate object. It is a horrifying idea.

In my loneliness, waiting around here all afternoon for Kirk to come back, I have been almost ready to panic. I thought of the horses, wanted to go see them. I was so disturbed that I started to the barn and was half way there before I remembered that Kirk had taken them both away yesterday and only brought the one back last night that he rode away today. Suddenly it occured to me that he might have taken them away to ground me. It sounds like a horrifying idea but I think it may be true and that, in itself, doesn't horrify me. It's funny why I trust Kirk so completely when every logical reason says I should not.

*   *   *

I have never known anything more welcome than the sound of horses hoofs yesterday and then the sight of Kirk riding up at a fast trot on one of the horses and leading the other. I couldn't run down the trail to meet him fast enough. It was glorious to see him and see his joy in seeing me. He is a man any girl would dream of, and it was ecstasy to know that the big light-up of his face came from seeing me. Without pulling up his horse he jumped off and hit the ground running toward me, grabbed me up in his arms and swung me around and around him. I cried with joy but my tears were lost in the merry-go-round of his arms.

The horses slowed to a walk then circled around and came back over to us. Kirk reached out a hand and held them. Then, with his other arm about me, we all went over to the barn to unsaddle the horses and turn them loose. I was so happy I was ready to jump out of myself. Then I began to wonder at the immense joy I felt at seeing the horses as well as Kirk. My thoughts turned back to my fears of being grounded and I asked him why he had taken them away.

"My reasons would take a long time to explain," he said. "Let's not go into it now. O.K.?"

He was in a very good humor. He seemed to feel as happy as I did. His voice laughed at me even through his matter of fact words. His words virtually confirmed my suspicions and it seemed worse when tacitly confirmed. But I didn't want to spoil the good feeling. I decided to let it pass.

"O.K." I said. "It doesn't matter now. You are back and the horses are back and I am happy."

Despite the black mood I had been in all afternoon I had dinner almost ready. By the time he had washed up I had the table looking beautiful and everything finished so it would need no further work on my part. I was terribly anxious to hear his voice and to talk myself but I kept my eagerness under control. We ate with the full attention to food and silent motions that has become more and more our custom since the first evening when I had him to dinner in my apartment.

15

That first evening in my San Francisco apartment he was silent for a long time as he watched me, then he told me I made a very beautiful art of serving dinner. I subtly invited comparison to the Japanese serving tea but he rejected the comparison. He said that was an accretion of many generations but mine was a personal choice and still had the vitality of its creator in it. I was so flattered and pleased that I have moved more and more in that direction in the time I have known him. And he has, by his attention, come to express more and more appreciation of each new innovation I make. Mostly I simply feel his appreciation; he seldom puts it into words.

If he had been a suave, smooth talking charmer I would have thought his first expressed appreciation was the fizz water of a smooth line. But there was nothing of the overly subtle woman-manipulator about him. Actually, except for a few occasions of surprisingly revealed sensitivity like that, I might have thought Kirk was a little dumb and unfeeling when I first met him. He had an intense reserve. There was something almost oriental about it. Now that I see so much oriental bloodlines here I wonder if he might not be part Chinese or Japanese. He is an inch or two over six feet and his eyes are almost blue, green with little brown specks in them, but I think he could have as much as an eighth Mongolian blood in him. There is also in him a hint of something that I think of as oriental ruthlessness. It's hard to define but it is something that might lead me to cast him as Genghis Khan in a play. Maybe instead of ruthlessness it's honesty. Maybe the two traits are really the same.

Honesty sounds strange applied to what I could actually tell about Kirk. He has hidden his past life from me completely. However, despite that, I feel that he is the most sincere and fully integrated person I've ever known. He *is* honest. His words are honest; his love is honest; his laughter and derision (and there is quite a lot of that) are honest. I know it; I feel it in every thing he does and says. I feel it when he touches me or holds me. It had to be that way. Otherwise I could never have committed myself to his world, totally unknown to me, just because it was his.

The commonplace simplicity of the events that started it all seem like something out of context when I ask myself where I am and what I'm doing here. I just went out in the warehouse one day to take a corrected bill of lading to a new truck driver who was making the Los Angeles run. It was a very ordinary thing for me to do. The dispatcher yelled at a man in the usual dark pants and leather jacket of a truck driver to "wait up." It was Kirk. He looked very ordinary; he was a handsome new guy I hadn't seen before but still a truck driver. He turned in my direction as I walked toward him. Of course, we looked each other over as every man and woman in their twenties look each other over from head to foot. But this was different. Something clicked. Before I was half way there our eyes met and my pulse said, "This is it; this is it; this is it." I'm not romantic and I don't believe in love at first sight. Maybe it was just sex but if so it was a new kind of sex — honest sex. He asked me then and there to have dinner with him the next night when he came back from L.A. He started by saying, "I want to know you" but he asked me for a date as simply as if we had always been friends. I accepted and less than two months later here I am.

The first thing strange that I noticed about Kirk was that his English contained some odd expressions. Pretty soon I found his knowledge of ordinary things had a lot of strange blank spots in it. Also he would tell me absolutely nothing about himself. At first I thought he might be an undercover agent of some foreign government. Then I realized he didn't have enough training in how an average American should behave to be a spy that wouldn't attract attention. He seemed never to have been around and picked up current slang and cliches of speech. He mentioned that he liked skiing then showed a complete ignorance of all ski resorts and called bindings "spring ski fasteners." I was always having to stop and translate such things as UN and NATO. After I did some checking on his job application with a girl who worked in our personnel office and told him what I had found out, he said it was all fiction — the whole thing. But he still refused to tell me anything about his past. Before then I used to press him about certain peculiarities of his English and his lack of knowledge of very ordinary things. "You must be a foreigner," I told him. "But if you're in the country illegally that seems no crime to me and I wouldn't cause you trouble about it. I might even be able to help you."

He didn't say simply, "No. I'm an American citizen, born in Podunk, Iowa" or something like that. I went over his words very carefully in my mind at the time and I remember them exactly. He said, "You may think my English isn't very good but I know no language other than the one I am trying to use. Also I am not a citizen of any foreign government."

That sort of thing became the routine of our relationship. He obviously wanted to relieve my fears about his strangeness but he wanted to follow a timing and purpose I didn't understand in telling me anything about himself. I have learned to accept this. I am still having to accept it. Maybe soon I will learn the reason for it. But it puzzles me even more now that I am here in an unknown place.

Last night I felt that he was very pleased about something; I felt that he would have something to tell me or show me. But as I have learned to do I waited — I didn't push him. We enjoyed being together and having dinner together. After dinner we had our coffee by the fireplace and he told me. It seemed very important to him but I am mystified as to why it should be. I've never won any popularity contests but I've always got along so well with everyone that I never thought much about it. And what he had to tell me seemed to be nothing more than this.

"Everyone loves you," he said. He said it with great enthusiasm. He said it as if, during all his unexplained absences, he had been taking a vital poll of opinion and was bringing me eagerly waited results. "Mostly they talk about how pretty you are." He went on. "There are not many blondes here and they talk a lot about your beautiful blond hair and blue eyes. And they talk about your wonderful figure. But they like the happy way you talk, and your sensitivity to each different person. You look at people, you know, as if each one were the whole world for you while you're looking at them. You look at old people like that and little children as well as handsome men."

I remembered the party and how happy I was and how many nice people were there. "All the people I've met here just happen to be very nice," I said. "I do like them and I guess it shows through. But I'm no Pollyanna. I don't like everybody. I don't want you to think I have an indiscriminate love that embraces the whole world. I don't."

"I know you don't," he said, and I knew he was telling me honestly something he had carefully thought about. "That's what I mean. You are intelligent and perceptive. When you look at someone you see *that* person. Most of the adults here have seen newsreels of zombi social affairs and receptions for royalty and political leaders in the world you came from. They've all been horrified by unsmiling smiles and unseeing eyes. Knowing that you came from zombiland they had steeled themselves for the first contact. But there is no one I have talked to who doesn't like you. Even Dag Angskuld. You remember the very tall, straight old man with the big scar across his cheek where a bear slashed him?" I said I did. "Dag has taken a new look at me because, as he said, 'I had the courage and the perception and' — these are his words — 'the love-making ability to bring you here.' "

He obviously wanted me to make some comment about Dag and I said, "I remember him very well. I saw him watching me a long time and then about the middle of the evening he came over very proudly and very courteously asked me to dance. He danced wonderfully well — he had regal grace in his proud dignity. He is every inch a king."

"He wouldn't be flattered by that appraisal," Kirk said, then regretted his words and added, "Let that remark pass, please. I'd rather not explain now. Did you truly like him?"

"Very, very much."

"Wonderful. That makes everything very good. He has not approved of me in the past but because of you he invited us to join the group he is in. It is the one I would have liked most but I would not have tried because I knew he would not accept me. Now we have been accepted."

I have written our conversation down, going over it in my own mind, and I still can't find why he was so surprised and happy that everyone should like me. I suppose every man feels that way to some extent about bringing home his bride but this seems more than normal. And then I have no idea whether I am accepted here as a bride or not. There has never been any marriage ceremony nor any mention of it between us. We spent our first night together about a week before Kirk asked me to come away with him and all thought of marriage that might have come up was pushed out by other events. Also no one has been introduced as Kirk's parents or family so there is no suggestion that our relationship might be socially disturbing. There are a lot of loose ends to be tied up but his attitude puzzles me.

He didn't really expect to be in this group we are going to be in and when I questioned him about it I gathered that it really doesn't mean very much. It seems to be a voluntary, and not necessarily permanent, grouping of people for the purpose of raising and storing food, exchanging tools, and otherwise carrying on the mechanics of living. Apparently there are a lot of such groups. They seem to be the usual way of life here. However not everyone belongs to one of them. We would have got along all right without any or had a choice of a dozen others. I gather that they are usually composed of about fifteen families.

Kirk used the phrase "about fifteen sovereigns." When I asked for a definition he told me that a full definition would have to wait awhile but from what he did tell me I picture a "sovereign" as a sort of family head, either a man or a woman. A sovereign might even be an orphaned child or a teenage boy or girl who wanted to sever relations with its parents. Kirk said that he is a sovereign but that I am not.

Tomorrow we are to meet the group as a group — apparently about half were at the party and I have already met them — and we are going to do some planting.

It sounds as if it might be fun and a good way to get acquainted but I still don't see why a prime qualification for a woman who is to be accepted as what sounds to me like a farm hand is that she be greatly loved by those with whom she is to work. Maybe there's something in Kirk's attitude that ties to the feeling I had about the children — something close to a fear of social ostracism.

My own fear of something approaching that came back to me for awhile today but not in the intensity I felt it yesterday. Kirk has gone away again today without telling me anything but that he would be back before sundown. He took only one horse today and when I got a touch of the loneliness panic I went out to see if he had left a bridle and saddle. He had and with the horse in the barn I felt less grounded.

Also I told Kirk about hearing a noise in the woods and asked him about a gun. He showed me a rifle very cleverly hidden as if having guns might be in violation of law. He said his grandfather had made the hiding place. He left the rifle out so I guess it is all right not to hide it. I didn't fire it but I showed him that I was well acquainted with its use.

The rifle is a 30-30 Winchester carbine. The brand looked dearly familiar. There is a good stock of ammunition that is also American made. The brand names did more to give me a feeling of security than the gun. I have become interested in the absence of brand names and looked the house over carefully without finding a single article that has a brand of any kind on it. There is hot and cold water but the fixtures in the kitchen and bath are of a strange design. They are very simple. They have no printing on them. They do not even say "Hot" and "Cold." They are almost unbelievably simple. I could repair anything myself. There is no electricity. So far I have not missed it; I love the candle light. Now that I think of it there was electricity in the big hall where we had the party. There is a big freezer well stocked with frozen food. The food is not in packages with brand names; apparently it was home packaged. I looked around and found that the refrigerator operates by a little flame burning oil or some liquid fuel.

I just realized that I am beginning to get a bonus enjoyment out of this. My purposeless writing (my screaming like a new born baby) is beginning to take the pattern of my first anthropological study. I guess that could have its bad points. If I should begin to look at people as an anthropoligist they might love me less. But the writing has suddenly given me a feeling of communicating with Professor Kane and for a moment I felt myself talking to a whole assembly, to all my old classmates reassembled to hear my penetrating analysis of a hitherto unknown civilization.

I don't know whether I like the idea or not.

No. I don't. I have come here with Kirk. I should accept his people as my people, not conjure up and try to relate to phantoms from the outside.

4.

I didn't understand before. I don't understand now. But I can see now that there is a very real lack of relation between this and the world I have known. Kirk's concern over my social acceptability as a farm hand by other farm hands was fully justified. My day of work in the field was the severest social test I have ever faced. And it was not because I ran into some tricky social idiosyncracies of peasants; there was none of the quaint, colorful provincialism that is slightly distasteful to me. This was something different from anything I had imagined. The plowing of manured fields was the setting of the most gracious behavior I have ever known, with everything done in a manner so natural and unobtrusive that no acknowledgement was ever made of the possible existence of anyone who had not undergone countless generations of good breeding. It was as if all the royal families of the world had come together to play at farming. The work simply brought everyone's attention into one focus and added the joy of robust physical activity — like skiing or riding to the hounds.

Funny, I felt the mood of things in the morning even before we got to the fields. Here everyone I have seen who was not walking was either on horseback or in a chariot behind two horses. We went to the welcoming party for me in a chariot. The fields where we were to work were not far but, because we wanted to use

21

the horses for plowing, Kirk harnessed them so he could just disconnect and connect to a plow. We were up early and he was ready with the chariot by the time I was through with the breakfast dishes. When I ran out and we started off the sun was just rising, there were a few clouds, the wind was blowing, the horses had been given grain and wanted to run and, because of the short distance, Kirk let them have their way. We went down the road through the woods at full gallop. It put me in a holiday spirit. That is the way it should have been. Everyone there obviously felt that working together was a sort of holiday.

When we first got there we found ten or twelve people with two horses already beginning work. The field was completely surrounded by woods like a mountain meadow — no buildings of any kind.

When we entered the clearing one of the girls in the group saw us and came running over calling our names and waving a greeting. As if our arrival was something especially important, two other girls detached themselves from the group and came running over too. They didn't saunter over like peasants tentatively approaching foreigners. They were anxious to see us and were self-assured enough to let their interest show freely. I remembered meeting the first one at the party but I didn't remember the other two and I'm very sure now that they had not been there. The three welcomed us as if they were the receiving line at a party and we the most wonderful of guests.

All three were very pretty and very different. Inger looked Scandinavian. Bingee was fair enough to have freckles but still had an oriental look about her. Lolena looked like an American Indian princess. They were all several years younger than I; the little freckled face Chinese girl called Bingee was not quite mature. But all of them had so much poise and self-assurance that it made them seem older. All were wearing what I would call sun suits of leather — short, sleeveless one piece outfits — exquisitely made but showing a lot of wear. With so much youth and beauty and warmth of greeting I had a moment of fear that this was why Kirk especially wanted in this group. The girls all knew our horses by name and welcomed them almost as warmly as they did Kirk and me. They told Kirk that someone wanted him in the "high" field. He left and they took possession of our horses and began unhitching them from the chariot as if by previous arrangement. At the same time they gave much attention to making me feel welcome.

I could soon see that the three girls were jointly in charge of

22

the work on this field. Apparently they knew from Kirk that I liked and could handle horses and it was an immediate bond between us. They took me in hand, introduced me to everyone there including two six or seven year old children, and said that the three of them and I would handle the horses.

It looked like a very inefficient operation to me from my little knowledge of farming but it developed that the horses did not often do this sort of thing and each one needed personal attention at first. Later in the day the person handling the plow also handled the horse or horses pulling it. Sometimes we hitched two horses together to one plow. Once for awhile we hitched four to one plow.

The attitudes of everyone toward the work puzzled me. Variety and experiment at the cost of efficiency seemed to be fully acceptable but I noticed that Inger was quite embarrassed and ashamed one time because she had shown poor judgment in one of the hookups she had requested. It was a tandem hookup between a single deep plow and a gang of six small light plows. The gang plows rode at a slant between plowed and unbroken land and covered up more than they turned over. Two men, much older and obviously much more experienced than she, had followed her instructions and helped her with the hookup without question. Afterwards they laughed and kidded her unmercifully about it but when she requested it they obeyed as if they were peasants and she royalty. Inger is Dag's daughter but apparently he is just one of the group. He doesn't seem to be in charge or have any special status.

These work relationships are going to take some getting accustomed to on my part. Instructions are issued as if by inherent right to command but the relationships are obviously temporary. If I think of it less as an employer-employee relationship and more as a host-guest, or in this case hostesses-guests, relationship I am able to understand it better. It seems to be something somewhere between that and an educational process.

I know very little about farming but from what I have seen in movies and newsreels this is a long way from usual present day farm methods. There are no tractors or heavy plows rolling up great ribbons of even textured earth. All the power is supplied by people and horses — not heavy draft animals but the same ones we ride. Ours and everyone's are fairly heavy-muscled, like quarter horses, but they have good gaits and good lines that in my mind definitely makes them riding instead of work horses. But the plows were small, no one expected more of them than the horses could pull, and the empathy between them and the people was so strong that I think the horses definitely enjoyed it.

In one way the use of riding horses for work seemed very appropriate to this place. I got a feeling that specialization — in horses, people, or anything — is looked upon with great disfavor here. People of all ages and both sexes took part in the planting indiscriminately.

There was apparent confusion that always gave way to a subtle order that I didn't fully understand. But definitely there was no secretiveness about the activity. There was none of the feeling of refusal to relate to the world I came from. Everything was quite different from my experience at the party. They were not relating to my world; I was relating to the world here; and I was accepted cordially. It was a wonderful feeling. I have never known such sincere acceptance in my life.

Everything is a puzzle just because it is so simple that the simplicity requires an explanation and I don't find one that satisfies me. The fields are just small clearings scattered through the woods. At some time during the winter division of responsibility for directing activity in each of the fields is decided on by some system of loose rotation. The desires and experience of each person seem to control. Actually I think maybe inexperience is more a determining factor than experience. I noticed that Dag, who apparently everyone honors for his experience and wisdom, never directed anything. He was often asked advice but he worked at some of the simplest tasks — breaking up weed roots with a hoe where the plows had not done a thorough job or throwing rocks to the edge of the field — things mostly done by the small children. The work relationship is intended to accomplish things but apparently the social side is the reason for group work.

There were four of us girls who started out handling the horses. Kirk had suggested that I wear a short corduroy skirt and sweater so I didn't feel out of place with my three leather-clad counterparts. In addition to the girls there were, in our field, two older men, one boy about the age of the girls who, of course, seemed quite a bit younger because boys mature later. Then there were two young men, a little older than I, who worked with great joy in muscular activity, or joy in showing off their strength. They seemed to have come courting and by the standards I know they were a little over attentive to me along with the three obviously prime targets. Of course I didn't mind. It may have been just their way of welcoming me. The two children and a man and woman in their thirties completed our immediate group. The man and woman, John and Pauline, were nice enough in their behavior but were of a coarser breed than the general run — both a little too fat, red faced and of a dirt farmer appearance. However, they were accepted fully by the others and the whole day had the feel of a picnic outing among beautifully behaved and thoroughly likable people.

There was an awful lot of singing. John and Pauline both had strong, full, robust voices that carried wonderfully in the fields. They sang with abandon as did everyone else. There were plenty of other things to think about besides singing but anyone would burst into song any time he felt like it. Sometimes there would be related answering songs from one side of the field to the other. Sometimes the same song was sung in parts. But everything was spontaneous. One sang or was silent as he felt like it.

The men paid their court mostly in song using the names of the girls — or my name — in most passionately revealing outbursts of emotion. A few of the songs were familiar to me, both the music and the words; and a lot of the music was familiar but the words were different from any I had heard. For example, one of the men sang "Rose Marie" with the words I know, but the theme song from "Oklahoma" had words about a mountain. Apparently people here don't relate to the world I have known even when they take songs from it. But there has to be a relationship of some kind if they take over songs. Very puzzling!

Late in the morning Inger said that everything was well in hand and told me she would like to take me around and let me meet all the others in the group. Two other fields were being worked that day. Both were bigger than ours but neither was big enough to really look like farm country; they were all just little clearings in the woods — no buildings. Everyone stopped work when we came up and took time to be friendly. It seemed a purely social occasion but at the same time everyone seemed greatly interested in the work. They talked about newly developed plows (all looked very simple compared to displays of farm machinery I had seen). They talked about methods of planting as if they were talking of a new grip for a tennis backhand or the condition of a golf course. Two fields were being planted to grain (one to oats and one to wheat) and one was being planted for hay — mixed grasses, peas, and clover. These things were discussed but these were not unimaginative farmers drolling cliches about the weather and crops over the fence. They were intelligent people who were interested in the wonder of what they were doing. It was almost as if creation of the world were something that had taken place only a few years ago and agriculture was still a novel experiment.

We ran into Kirk in one of the fields. He was handling a plow with two horses and was stripped to the waist and glistening with sweat. He seemed to have an interest far greater than the occasion called for in how I was enjoying myself. I was enjoying myself immensely and said so. I guess I showed it. It seemed to make him very happy. He asked Inger for her opinion of my ability. She said I was very good with the horses. I suppose I deserved the blank left by what she failed to say. It was very conspicuous but I don't think she thought of being unkind, just honest. I know I was pretty bad at the work; I was so bad that no one would ridicule me.

About half a mile from the last field, almost fully in the woods — very little clearing around — we came to a log house, Hellstroms,' that was being used as a base for preparing food for all the people working. The women with little babies seemed to be the ones preparing food; there was quite a nursery activity in one room. In the kitchen six or seven women were bustling around like movies of an old fashioned farm at threshing time. However, even here, when I was introduced all around, no one was too busy to be gracious. Word had already been sent out that the meal was ready, so Inger and I were pressed into service to help get everything put on tables out under the trees.

The food was simple, good, and plentiful. There were three tables. At a glance I equated the three tables with the three fields and work groups but apparently there was a deliberate intent to give companions different from the ones with whom we had been working. The women who had prepared the food took their places at the tables, decisively took over the roles of hostesses, and seated everyone. No one waited on the tables; all food had already been put on.

The lunch turned out to be a long luncheon in which discussion seemed purposeful. It lasted from about midday until well into the middle of the afternoon. Conversation never lagged. These were discussions by people interested in what they were talking about. All of them expressed their points of view effectively. The tables were well enough separated so that voices didn't carry from one to another and the discussion, at least at our table, was general. The day's activity and food growing were tossed around without apparent direction for awhile and then our two hostesses seemingly became joint moderators, subtly steering the discussion from one subject of *their* selection to another. The methods and activities of our group were often compared to those of other groups but from very surprising perspectives. Work efficiency was occasionally considered but the relationship between man and the earth and other living things was part of everyone's thought pattern. The viewpoint was almost pagan at times but it really seemed to be more of a cross between a religious and artistic attitude. There was nothing that was either religious or artistic in the sense that I have known these things but there was an interest in more than the superficial significance of our activities. There was much I didn't understand but frequently my presence was acknowledged by an explanation made especially for me and I was invited to ask questions. Twice my questions were countered by saying that a full answer would have to await my further acquaintance but I confined all questions to things that were being discussed and no one told me he didn't relate to the things I brought up.

I've decided that the apparent slide back into the simple rural life of the nineteenth century is a surface similarity only, but I'm not sure yet just what to think of the whole experience.

5.

Definitely, there's something very unsimple about the simplicity here. From the day I spent with the children I'm convinced that attitudes are firmly grounded and continuing — that this is not merely some obscure cult of sophistication-weary intellectuals who have joined together and gone part way back to the life of the "noble savage." My imagination is not wild enough for me to think I have been reincarnated with these people into the embryo of something like a Greek city-state after the cycle of time has passed through the rise and fall of the atomic age. But sometimes it seemed like that on our day of planting. Conversation at the lunch seemed to take in full knowledge and judgment of everything I have learned about the people all over the world for the past ten thousand years. And here everyone talks as if they had first name acquaintance with people of all time and had seen them yesterday or day before — certainly no later than last year.

During the long luncheon they talked about Ho Sin (or some such Chinese sounding name) and John, who were working out a smelting process in an old building somewhere. From the tone I suspect it was within walking distance. There was no reference to the massive factories elsewhere and the millions of tons of fine steel being made.

Then our use of horses was reexamined as if domestication of horses was a new and controversial issue. Mention was made of one group (members were called by name and in answer to my inquiry I was assured that I could get to the valley under discussion in half a day on horseback) where cheese made from mare's milk is a stable of diet as is horse flesh. The horse eating people were criticized, not because they used horses for food, but because they used them for food and also trained them for riding. There was one voice of dissent at our table but everyone else agreed that riding was too great an intimacy to establish with an animal one was going to eat; the two relationships confused the emotions. Another group worked cattle to plows and also ate them but usually not the same animals. Another group ate no domestic animals — apparently because of the work required to feed and care for them. One family mentioned was clearly in what I would have called the hunter-food-gathering stage. The family was obviously well-known and socially acceptable. They apparently chose their way of life with deliberation when other ways were open to them and their choice was respected. Never was any of the other groups mentioned with condescension. Their way of doing things was examined and the cause for rejecting it turned over anew — as if the results of the last ten thousand years of mankind's experience were either unknown or considered so inconclusive that it would be naive to mention them.

The two hostesses at my table were clearly steering conversational subjects with the same imperial, but presumably temporary, command-of-the-situation that the girls exercised in the field. It was not conspicuously done but I sensed and was flattered that some of the things were discussed especially for me.

One point that I would have liked to know more about was not clarified for my benefit — the relationship between the sexes. I picked up a very definite impression that women do not work with men because of an attempt to ignore differences. They do the same work because it is accepted as axiomatic that no one can be free and independent who is not capable of independent survival, and the capability for independent survival seems to be *at least one* of the prime concerns of the people here. A woman as well as a man is expected to have demonstrated that capability — not simply have the potential — and a child is expected to demonstrate it as early as possible.

As to what the socially approved relation between the sexes is

28

I am completely at sea. There was mention made of a woman "accepting" a man or having children by him but I suddenly realized the word "marriage" was never used. I wanted to ask about it but I didn't. Because I didn't know how my relationship with Kirk might be looked upon, I thought I might be skating on thin ice, so I kept quiet on the subject and listened. The word was never used. Neither was the word "husband" or "wife." Father, daughter, mother, son, sister, brother — but never husband or wife.

In school I was taught that there has never been a society that did not recognize marriage of some kind; even what looks like free love to monogamous people is always recognized as group marriage. If an intellectual people become completely free from the savage's fear of incest, one might think of a society with no concept of marriage, but it would be hard to imagine. I certainly don't think a completely open, sexually promiscuous society is what exists here. But what does exist is a total mystery to me.

When I began to look for the word "marriage" or something that would pass for it in the luncheon conversation I almost lost interest in everything else. I focused for awhile on the point like a detective looking for clues. But it did no good. The word lover was sometimes used but, although babies and fathers were often mentioned, neither the word marriage nor the tone implying its absence was ever used.

When we went back to work in the fields my interest was greatly aroused and I studied the behavior between men and women, especially the ardent court the young men were paying to the three girls and, I thought, also to me, and I found a delicate balance of restraint — as if some obscure social taboos were fully respected. My curiosity became too strong and I had to ask Kirk about it last night.

I realized that it was on the border line of talking to him about the world I had known, which I had agreed not to do for a month. But in another way it was just trying to learn the acceptable language. So I said, "No one ever uses the word marriage here and I have never found a word that is used in its place. What word does one use when he wants to talk of the marriage relationship."

I felt that he looked at me a little disappointed as if he thought I had gone back on my promise, but maybe it was my imagination. He was slow in answering and for a moment I thought he was going to say "I don't relate to marriage." Almost he did but, at least, he used different and less blunt words.

"There *is* no word because what you call the marriage relationship doesn't exist here."

"But what about our relationship?"

"Our relationship is unique. There's no other like it here."

I stared at him uncomprehendingly, then decided he meant that I didn't yet belong — that I was somehow foreign and still beyond full acceptance on a normal basis.

"But people live together in the same house, and a man and woman sleep in a single bed and perform sexual acts that result in the woman having a baby. That is the relationship I want a word for."

He smiled and gave a little derisive snort. He was laughing at my excessive seriousness, I guess. But his face became serious again.

"That's not marriage," he said. "You know horses have the same relationship and you don't use the word marriage when you talk about it."

He saw that I was stymied without referring to the world I had known and decided to at least throw me a crumb of relating to it.

"You know some words for the simple relationship you describe but most of them, when used in connection with human relations, have dirty connotations, even the formal word fornication. Marriage is not a word for the simple relationship you describe and it is not a word for the more complex relationship between you and me, nor for the sort of relationship that usually develops between men and women here.

"There is no word for marriage here. If there were it would be something with an undesirable connotation like whore, another word that you know but won't run into here."

"Whore and marriage mean opposite things," I protested. "Or at least they are on opposite sides of the fence."

"They don't seem so to me," he said. "And they wouldn't to most people here if they knew them. A whore negotiates for a single short sexual relationship. In marriage both the man and the woman negotiate the relationship, have and proclaim extraneous considerations in the ceremony, and even make and record a formal contract. Social approval of this contractual relationship is also part of the meaning of the word marriage. No *contractual* sexual relationship of any kind has social approval here. If there existed such a relationship here our society would look upon it as something shameful, and if there were a word for it, it would be a dirty word."

I was flabbergasted — partly at so many words from Kirk and

partly at what he was saying. I guess I looked flabbergasted.

"Don't try to rush it," he said. "I think a month should give you a clear enough idea of our life here for you to decide whether or not you like it."

We got back to good terms and I guess it was not a real break of faith on my part. Anyway Kirk didn't seem angry.

Maybe I shouldn't rush it but now my curiosity is really aroused. There's something here in the relationship between man, woman, and society in general that either eludes me so completely that I must be awful dumb, or else it has never before existed in the history of the world — at least, not as I learned that history.

6.

Bit by bit I am putting the pieces together but they still don't make a very definite pattern.

I can see that Kirk is paving the way for letting me into the community life here in a gradual manner that will give me time to digest it. But his absences, I find, have also another motivation. He has been away from here about a year. I try very hard to hold to my promise not to talk about the outside world, so I haven't asked him where he was before he became a truck driver in San Francisco four months ago. But because of the long absence he now feels some sort of need to go around and reacquaint himself with everyone. "It is cowardly to isolate oneself," he said.

Apparently the same motive of avoiding cowardly behavior prompted him to take me on an extensive get-acquainted tour the day before yesterday. It was obvious that he had already paved the way by his visits alone; everywhere we went he had been seen since his return and everyone was expecting me. I can't see why any special courage is required to meet people here; everyone, without exception, is extremely courteous. Some are very reticent, and some are a little stiffly formal, but many are cordial. All have friendly attitudes and are well-mannered.

We met again the fine old man who said the first night at the party that I seemed to be coming out of my zombi state "quite well." His name is Hans Hargrave. He seems to be engaged in some scholarly work at a low, one story, stone building of some sort that contains a library. It would be a small building in San Francisco, but for here it is big. We didn't go in the library portion. I was curious to see what sort of books are there if people don't

31

relate to the outside world, but I didn't get a chance. I will soon I suppose; I certainly want to get to know Hans better and he asked me to visit him there any time I liked.

There are a lot of people I want to know here and most of those I especially liked asked me to call. But I suppose I should follow Kirk's lead and get the general feel of things before I go wandering off on my own. The apparent fear of ostracism, the unmistakable orientation on individual independence, and the stated concept that too much isolation is cowardly need some digesting before I can see how they fit together. There must be some more pieces to the jigsaw puzzle that I haven't seen yet.

In my tour I found a lot of evidence that, in addition to whatever more subtle factors may exist here, this society is geared positively and consciously to individual independence. Physical isolation even seems highly prized. There was one big rambling old house in a clearing with three smaller houses grouped around to form a sort of court. All were in use and several people, ten or eleven, came from the places to meet us in the living room of one of the smaller houses into which we were first invited. But aside from that one group of houses each house I saw was in a separate clearing not visible from any other.

None of the houses was very big or elaborate. Two were actually caves in the hillside. But everything was substantially built. Even the caves were permanent stone work. Stone and logs are generally used on the outside of the houses but milled lumber is sometimes used and allowed to weather. I saw no paint anywhere except in two places where there were decorative designs around the doors as in Scandinavian countries. The interiors were all well finished like ours and like ours the finely sanded wood was always oiled instead of being painted or varnished.

There is no town in the usual sense. I saw again the big hall where we had my reception party. No other buildings are in sight of it. The building containing the library is alone. We went in what was called a smelter and steel foundry but it was a small isolated place with about twenty men, women, and children working. It was not an industrial plant as I know industry. There was another place where wood fiber was being processed into cloth. Everything there looked like it was on a small experimental scale but they obviously did not consider it a pilot operation for a larger plant. I was assured that usable quantities of synthetic fiber were produced with less effort and no more complicated tools than the same amount of wool from sheep or the same amount of flax could be turned into thread for cloth. I counted only fifteen people there but even so, as they explained the operation to me, they made it clear that they wanted to reduce it in size so it would be simpler to set up.

After the "foundry" we visited the one store that is available to everyone here. That certainly seemed simple enough. I feel that there may be something a little odd about the selection of merchandise offered for sale but I am not sure. Maybe the people here just have different tastes from those elsewhere.

At first glance it looked very ordinary and very much like what I expected after visiting around the area. I thought it could pass for a movie set of a Hudson Bay Trading Post or a general merchandise store in a pioneer western town. It was a big warehouse sort of building and there were a lot of tools, saws, axes, hoes, picks — a lot of them used — bins of nails and all such things. There were bolts of drab looking cloth and the smell of leather and harness oil.

Bingee, the very young, freckled face, Chinese looking girl I had worked with in the field, was a salesgirl in the store. She seemed to be expecting me and hurried over with a welcoming smile when we came in. She had on a brown blouse, a bright colored print skirt, a wide leather belt, bare legs and sandals. Her hair was tied back with a bright band that matched her skirt. She looked very pretty.

An old man also was working there. She took us over and introduced him and me; Kirk had obviously seen him the day before. The man was grey and a little bent over but fairly alert and friendly. He said the same thing that people frequently say to me here, that he had heard about my arrival and had been wanting to meet me and that I was even prettier than I had been described. He could have passed for the store's proprietor in a western movie set but I learned that "no one owns the store" and that he and Bingee and other clerks work on a rotating basis. "Almost everyone does at some time," Bingee told me. "You'll probably want to do it sometime, yourself. You spend all day meeting different people, learning what they are doing, and what they need."

"Do you get paid for working," I asked.

She said she did but didn't mention any amount and seemed to consider the payment unimportant but the experience good.

As we talked and walked around I tried to imagine myself showing Bingee through a big department store in San Francisco. At first I got a picture of that little round, freckled, slant eyed face lighted up with ecstatic delight but the more we talked the more I began to wonder if she would not walk slowly around in a puzzlement gradually becoming tinged with contempt. Then I tried to imagine contempt from her and could not. But the picture of Bingee delighted with all the wonders in a department store wouldn't come back to me. Everyone knows a woman likes pretty things. I do; I have never met one who didn't; and Bingee is no exception. But I am sure that a profusion of pretty things offered for sale in a department store would not make her ecstatic. She would question why there was so much and unless she got a satisfactory answer she would not accept the whole. It might not be easy to answer her questions. I realize that training and reasoned judgment of some kind is behind her attitude but I can't quite grasp it — even though something almost graspable about it plays at the edge of my consciousness.

I have read about the Indians of the Pacific Northwest who acquired great wealth and money or some sort of symbols of great wealth, then gave them to their enemies to insult them, or dropped them in the ocean to demonstrate a contempt for wealth. I remember that our teacher at the U commented that it was nothing different, the same old status game of wealth grabbing, just conspicuous destruction instead of conspicuous consumption. Maybe his explanation was just a little too simple.

The only other parallel that I can remember is the life of the Spartans. Of course, talking of Spartan simplicity is the commonest of cliches, but when I read about Lycurgus I got something approaching understanding out of it, I think. As I remember the enforced Spartan simplicity tended to concentrate on the development of the people and their behavior instead of focusing on material wealth and possessions. But if I remember right, in Sparta it was all for a military purpose and that apparently is not the case here.

I might be able to see the attitude here (I take it that Bingee represents the general attitude) as a reaction of an intellectual or artistic group to the pressures of TV commercials and the rest of the buildup but I feel sure that these people have been here since long before TV or even radio. It may be that they see the hunger for gadgets as the root of the "zombi" way of life and in guarding against "zombiism" they feel that they have to guard against the roots from which it springs. Anyway when we were leaving the store I had a sudden feeling that I was a zombi who had just run a test maze and my reaction was of interest to the observers.

The old clerk (I think his name was Roland but I don't know

whether that was a first or last name) looked at me curiously when we started to leave and asked, "Is there anything we don't have here that you couldn't make for yourself or couldn't be happy without?"

Although the same idea had been going through my mind all the time I was there I was not fully prepared to make a considered final conclusion and I felt that was what was being asked of me. I hesitated a moment. I felt Bingee and Kirk and the old man come together like three scientists observing the reaction of a rare specimen to some experiment. They waited intently for my words. I wanted to scream out, "Don't look at me like that. I'm not some freak. I'm just like you. Don't isolate me." (I didn't think of it at the time but my feelings could have been expressed by the classic words of Shylock: Have I not eyes, hands, senses, affections, passions the same as you? Am I not fed by the same food, hurt with the same weapons, warmed and cooled by the same summer and winter? If you tickle me will I not laugh, if you prick me will I not bleed, if you poison me will I not die?)

However I answered lamely and calmly, maybe with the routine reaction a zombi has learned for such occasions, "I haven't felt any need for anything I don't have since I have been here. I can see that I'm going to need to learn some skills, learn to do a lot of things I never thought about before, but I guess I can. It could be a lot of fun."

I'm sure my reaction could not have been more disappointingly bland but the tension passed — the three scientists again became Kirk, Bingee, and a slightly bent old man selling new and second-hand tools. We came home and while Kirk unsaddled and fed the horses I made dinner. Things seemed different. I looked at the dishes, the handmade table and chairs, the hand woven table spread, the candles, the ceramic candlesticks, the house and everything in it with new eyes. I looked at each thing and thought about how much work had gone into everything's making. I looked again at the food freezer and later asked Kirk about it. It was handmade locally. He and his grandfather and the clerk in the store, Roland, made it about eight years ago. It can run on any fuel that will supply a small heat source, even a candle.

Ever since the store I have been going over everything I can think of and measuring its value to me and thinking of the things that are important that I may need to learn to make. Kirk knows a lot about how things are made here. Of course, I know he knows about all sorts of things that are not here; he worked and lived in

San Francisco as well as somewhere else outside. But if I forget and talk about something that is not here he asks where I saw that and I have to back down because of my promise. It has become a joke between us because always, when he asks, I stop and think, laugh, and say, "I guess I dreamed it."

7.

My feelings about this place vacillate a lot. Sometimes I feel as if I had been reincarnated in another period of time. But there is difficulty in identifying the time. In some ways my day of work in the field was very close to a day on a big family farm in the early nineteenth century. Then sometimes it seems to go back to early pioneer days of inexperienced settlers with great hopes for a glorious future. Then other times it oscillates between a feeling of remote primitiveness and a futuristic time when the world may be rebuilt on the ruins of what I know by people having more taste and greater intelligence. No known parallel seems quite right.

I have been looking for a concept of something comparable that has been playing at the edge of my consciousness and I think I have it. It is the physicist's theory that the existence of matter implies the existence of negative matter. This seems to be a society whose impulse is the reverse of the civilization I have known. Everyone seems to be cooperating with a goal of removing the need for cooperation.

As evidence, there was the expressed wish for a simpler operation that would require the cooperation of fewer people in both the steel foundry and the synthetic textile plant. We also visited a glass producing plant where I got the same idea. But the store, more than the "factories" or anything I have seen made me realize the great difference between this and a typical western frontier town when the United States was being settled.

When Bingee told me about the rotation of the clerks I imagined a sort of cooperative jointly owned by the community in which all members rotated the work at a nominal wage. But as she showed me around and talked about what we were seeing, differences from my ideas of the place began to show up. The merchandise for sale was fairly commonplace but the ideas about buying and selling seem to be the reverse of those that I have known.

There was none of the usual pride that exclaims, "We are a pioneer country but we are making progress. Our store is better

36

stocked all the time. We are beginning to get imports from all over the world. Almost anything you want could be bought here."

Instead Bingee had a note of shame that the meager selection of goods was so extensive. It was faint but still clearly defined. Showing me the display of new tools she said, "It's not easy for each man to make his own and since most people's way of life is built around the use of these tools we stock and sell them."

Then she showed me some used tools and said of one bunch, "John Haugland bought more than he really had to have and brought these back for resale." Of another bunch she said with admiration, "Richard Wing, from the other side of Stone Mountain, brought these in and said, 'Sell them to some uneducated person. I have learned to live without them."

Of a stack of beautifully finished pieces of leather, mostly full hides, she said, "Most people have a surplus of these and we take them in trade on cloth and keep them in stock so that everyone is constantly reminded that cloth is something we could do without."

Then she showed me some cloth and said, "Most of the cloth is brought in. We used to need it for clothes before we learned simple ways of tanning leather but no one has really needed it for a long time. There are a lot of different kinds made from trees and plants. We bring all varieties in mostly to learn about them."

I asked where they were brought from. She answered simply "zombiland" and, as if not to dwell on the shame of my origin, went on talking about synthetics without a pause.

"Some people," she said, "think that ways can be developed to produce synthetic cloth easier than leather. Synthetics can already be made easier than cloth from wool or flax. They are being made by the people who don't eat domestic animals and so don't have much leather. We may someday fit them into our way of life. In many ways they are not as good as leather but they are easier to sew and one can have fun making a lot of clothes with little effort." Then she added with a world weary shrug that seemed funny coming from a young girl in a simple print skirt, "Of course, if you have too many changes of pretty clothes they lose their dearness."

While she was talking I had been looking at the cloth. There was a very wide selection of materials, especially in the cloth that had been "brought in." It was all good. The quality seemed exceptionally high. I found myself feeling the textures of each piece. Maybe I was responding to Bingee's lead. I remember how sensually her fingers played with the materials. Maybe my intense appreciation of texture was because of the lack of patterns. Every piece was either white or some muted solid color. There were no patterns anywhere. I remembered my welcoming party and all the variety of colorful clothes. I asked Bingee why there were no patterns. She didn't seem to understand, then I admired her skirt and asked her why there were no beautiful patterns like that.

When the idea was clear to her she tried to give me a simple honest answer to what I soon understood was an embarrassing question because it marked me as a zombi. She said no one would bring back for resale a piece of cloth after printing one's own pattern on it. I asked her if she had printed her own. "Of course," she assured me. "Didn't you print yours?" I was wearing a print blouse. I told her that I not only didn't print it but didn't even sew it, that I bought it in a store already made."

Her silence while she digested the information and decided what she could say about it without being unkind was the sort that might have met me outside if I had said it was a handout from a charity organization. She decided to say nothing and, to cover the embarrassing moment, began showing me colors, silk for screening, and comparing for me the relative virtues of silk screening and block printing. "In the winter it is a lot of fun," she assured me. "When it rains it's cozy to stay indoors and make pretty things."

She showed me bins of dry paint pigments, barrels of bulk paint vehicles and a great variety of dyes. "We have a lot of this stuff," she said. "Some is found here and we are getting more and more recipes for making it. A lot is being made here now. However there's no need to stop imports of this. Everyone considers that it doesn't endanger our way of life to bring in this sort of thing because no one becomes dependent on it."

There were also many bins of bulk beads, enormous spools of various size wires of gold, silver, copper and brass colors apparently sold by the yard. "Some people like to make jewelry and such things in the winter. Almost everyone thinks it is better to have a lot of supplies available so no one will feel that jewelry is something precious."

"Don't you like jewelry?" I asked.

"Oh yes. I think it adds a festive feeling for everyone to wear lots of colorful jewelry at a dance. And sitting around making it brings on memories of the fun at the last party or plans for the next one. It's just like dying your clothes or making prints on them. You try to show how you feel inside and then it's a lot of fun looking at how all the others say they are feeling. There are a lot of surprises at every party."

"Does no one make jewelry or clothes for anyone else?"

"Sometimes. But when others try to tell you how they think you usually don't feel that way at all. It's good to understand what they think but it's sometimes very sad when it's something you don't like. Of course, if someone understands you well enough to give your feelings a little push in the direction you want to go it is a wonderful floating feeling."

Kirk and the other clerk, the old man, had started out to accompany Bingee and me on our look around but a customer came in and both went back to talk to him. When he left they didn't rejoin us. I have learned that although everything seems very casual everyone's actions here usually show up later as having been deliberate and purposeful. I wondered if I were left alone with Bingee purposely and why. All I could think of was that there could be no better form of communication between two worlds than to put a woman from each in one of their stores together. I assumed that was what was happening and fell in with the idea by asking Bingee endless questions about everything that I could think of buying that she might "relate to."

There was a big supply of knives, guns, rifles, pistols, and a large stock of ammunition.

"Are these part of the way of life here?" I asked.

"The knives are," she said. "A few hunters use guns but most people who live by hunting prefer to use traps of their own making or weapons that don't scare away the animals — bows and arrows and blow darts. We bring in the guns so that everyone can have them and be familiar with their use in case some unexpected trouble should develop and guns might come as a surprise."

Her meaning was not clear to me but I didn't want to ask her if she meant they were to protect from an invasion by zombis. I am not by any means sure that she did.

There was a stock of coffee, tea, tobacco, and spices which seemed to have a position in her mind somewhere between jewelry materials and firearms — harmless because not necessities but good things to be familiar with.

I saw no other groceries and since I had learned that there was no other store I asked her if they didn't sell food.

It seemed to impress her as being a very strange question. She had to think about it. "No one sells food," she said at last. "It's a basic necessity. Everyone grows, or hunts, or gets his own some way for himself."

"But what of people who are doing other work, or who have

bad luck or get sick or hurt and can't work?"

She looked at me trying to comprehend my reason for asking the question. She was never catty, or fighting a foreign attitude as peasants do. She was sincerely interested in seeing my point of view and in explaining her own. "If you have food and you like the people who need some you give them some," she said. "If you know someone you don't like then, of course, you would like to see them starve."

The attitude was a little difficult for me to reconcile with Bingee's graciousness and with the graciousness of everyone I have met here. The thought went through my mind that there might be a concept inverse to the broad love of humanity which accentuates personal graciousness. I wanted to explore the idea but I decided not to introduce further incongruous ideas. Instead I strengthened my resolve to respect my hostess' plans of the moment. These appeared to be some sort of education in what is considered a proper thing to sell in a store and what is not.

I learned that furniture one made for oneself. I recalled the good but simple furniture of well sanded and well oiled wood in our own house which Kirk had told me was made mostly by his grandfather who is now dead. I wondered what sort of place we would have if Kirk had had to make the house and all the furniture himself. But such things last hundreds of years and can be accumulated slowly.

I recalled our beautiful blue earthenware dishes and, seeing nothing of the sort about the store, asked Bingee about dishes and cooking utensils.

In her view dishes are not a necessity and they are not sold as art materials because they are finished art themselves. She said the activity of making dishes was good because clay was fun to handle and the use of common kilns brought people from different groups together who didn't ordinarily get a chance to work with each other.

Metal cooking utensils are sold. They are a problem yet to be solved, she said, like tools. They are still part of the way of life and difficult for each person to make for himself. They are all made locally now but the plant has to be too big, the process takes too long, and requires the coordinated effort of too many people who have to make a long study of "the recipes."

"If someone else would grow their food for them so they could give all their time to it," I asked her, "wouldn't that be all right?"

"It takes much too long," she insisted, "sometimes years. If we

40

made metal as good as that brought in it would take even longer. The people making it would become specialists." Her inflections were very subtle but I clearly understood that a specialist was either immoral, physically repulsive, or both.

I think that contempt for the idea of a specialist as opposed to a respect for specialists in the outside world may be the big clue to the difference of attitude. There is no fanatical love of "the noble savage" here, and there is no reverence for asceticism. People here like material things; perhaps in comparison to the people on the outside they even have a greatly heightened appreciation of them. There is a sort of Greek like sensuality in their love of food and drink and contact with the physical world. But they want to know where everything comes from and, if their way of life is dependent on it, they want to be able to produce it. Specialization is out. If the effort of producing a thing is a pleasant experience, like working in the fields, making dishes, or clothes, or jewelry then the product is not only good in itself but good because of the activity that goes into its production. Then each person wants to do it for himself. If the activity of a thing's production is not good — if it is tedious, monotonous, or takes up a disproportionate amount of time — no one wants it because he makes himself dependent on the sort of tiresome or dull people who produce it; he develops an obligation to persons he doesn't like. The activity of doing things together, without creating permanent interdependence, is chosen for social enjoyment.

I can see something behind the point of view. Specialists are usually respected in the outside world but, after all, they do either evolve from the practice of slavery or from the practice of making places in society for persons who don't have the temperament or ability to live well-rounded lives. I suppose, if there is not going to be an aristocracy built on a slave society, people have to either specialize and become increasingly dependent on each other, or choose a well-rounded life and pay whatever the cost in foregoing the sort of wealth that is measured in gadgets. The people here seem to have made a choice and made it with full awareness of what they were doing.

8.

I realize that Kirk has been making things very easy for me by thoughtful planning, but yesterday he seemed to want to make things very hard and drive home my new knowledge that I can't run down to a store and buy everything I want. We spent the day alone together planting a garden. It was hard work with hand tools. Pretty monotonous too. I got very tired, but Kirk said it doesn't take many days like that to grow all the grain and vegetables two people need for a year. I didn't realize that a space about the size of two city lots (They use metric measurements here and I am going to have to learn them.) will grow enough grain for a thousand loaves of bread. When I think of it that way I guess I accomplished quite a lot yesterday. We are only growing a little grain "to keep in practice doing things for ourselves." We will have all the grain we need from our share of the group work.

Today Kirk has gone off again. Maybe he's giving me another digestion period for my new experiences and maybe he's giving me a chance to get the kinks out of my muscles. I need it for both.

* * *

I'm not quite sure why I want to write all these things down but I do. Maybe I'm just like a baby screaming as I said when I first started — although I no longer feel like screaming. Maybe they will be good to look back on after I find out what this place is really like. And maybe I think I am a great scientist who has made a big discovery of an unknown civilization or something. Anyway I keep on doing it, trying to get down everything significant.

I just remembered something that I should get down for future analyzing; it doesn't mean anything yet. Just before we started to leave the store, and Bingee and I came back to where Kirk and Roland were, I saw a slip of paper on the counter with a bolt laying on it to hold it down. I suspected that it was payment for the saw or whatever it was the customer bought while Bingee and I were looking around. I tried to be casual but I also tried to get a good look at it. It had the words "Camp 38" on it and the figure "20." There was no designation — dollars, yen, mark, or anything — to indicate what was the unit of currency.

Later I asked Kirk about it but he said that it would be better if I didn't know more about it just yet. Obviously whatever is used for money here would be a clue to how "here" is tied to the "outside."

I wonder if, instead of being a cooperative store, Camp 38 can be a camp of a mining, lumber, or scientific research company and the store be a company store. I have certainly seen no indication that anything is produced here that would form the basis for a "balance of trade" with the "outside." But also I see nothing being done here that would be of value to a mining, lumber, or scientific company able to pay for the materials that "are brought in." Very puzzling.

9.

How insensitive I have been! I have been focusing on my own aloneness and been completely blind to the aloneness of the man who held me close in his protecting arms. Suddenly last night I learned that this is no parlor game Kirk is playing by established rules, while friends well familiar with the rules look on. This is no game with friends ready to cheer a well patterned conformity or laugh good humoredly at some petty mistake. There was significant meaning behind his saying that it is cowardly to live alone. Somehow, for some reason, Kirk has been wandering between the heaven and hell of two worlds, as if the heaven and hell of one world were not enough, and he has brought me back into this one. I am a zombi shown two worlds by a Pygmalion and asked to choose, when the request is a prayer that the zombi will become a woman.

Why should Kirk bring me here when there were already Inger and Lolena? Was it love of me? In the religions of zombiland, did God become man to save man or because a heaven full of angels is a lonely place?

Pygmalion? God? Am I making something of Kirk beyond that which he is? Why do I grasp at religious thoughts for which I have before only felt contempt? "All this talk of pot and potter. Who's the potter, pray, and who the pot?"

But what I have just learned about Kirk and my relationship to him is something of utmost importance. It makes me reach for thoughts I never had before — makes me examine my scraps of fundamental knowledge. I've always been an agnostic and now I need something behind the facts. I need to examine volition and intent. In the bubbling primordial ooze, when the first organism separated into male and female, which created the other and why? Did man create woman or woman man? Did Eve eat of an apple and give a bite to Adam? Or were man and woman created by drinking from one cup of volition, each offering to each, and holding the cup to the other's lips?

Last night again I was offered a choice of two worlds, a choice that was no longer between a known and an unknown but between two worlds that had at least been glimpsed. I was not actually holding in my hands sleeping pills and a cup of coffee as I did before, but that is what it would have been if I had asked for it. Kirk offered to give me something to knock me out with the understanding that I would wake up again in my old apartment in San Francisco. I could then consider the past two weeks as a vacation or a dream — better a dream, he said, because no one would believe me. I wouldn't see him again and would never know where I'd been.

He was not just asking, "Do you regret coming? Would you like to go back?" He was not asking questions to be considered with only a remote possibility that they might lead to serious decisions. This was a deadly serious offer that called for an immediate, unequivocal choice. It was something he had been working to make possible all the time by keeping from me the knowledge of where we are and other things "that it would be better for me not to know just yet."

The choice was no problem for me. Before Kirk no one anywhere meant anything to me except Peggie and she has her own life to live. When I came with Kirk I was choosing him — not a world — choosing with a "whither thou goest I will go" attitude.

But last night I had a feeling that such a choice is no longer good enough. I felt that Kirk, who had been carrying me, sat me down on my own feet and was eager to see if I could stand and walk on them.

Even though the agreed month was only about half gone, he relieved me of my promise not to talk about the world I had known. He wanted to hear the things I had liked in each and know how I rated the two worlds side by side. He was very much afraid that the tinsel and gadgetry I had left were more important to me than they are. He had decided that these things might be more important to me than anything else and he thought I had now seen enough to face a now or never decision about returning. He wanted me to make such a decision without waiting to learn about underlying social concepts and motives that make this place what it is.

We talked for three or four hours. It was a much more serious and sustained discussion of big ideas than we ever had before. My head is spinning from the things I learned about him and this place. If I had heard the same things from anyone else I would have thought I was talking to a madman. I might think so now if I had not been here and met dozens of people, who "don't relate" to what has always been the "normal" world as I knew it. But having

44

been here and having learned that Kirk is the solidest person I have known in two worlds, when he said seemingly absurd things I knew I had to believe him.

It was not easy. If he had been telling me about fantastic mechanical wonders I would have had no trouble believing him. They would have given me a feeling that this world is built of different substance and is subject to different truths. But mechanically this world is very ordinary. Outwardly it is much less spectacular than the world I left. The things he told me were hard to believe because he was talking about men and women doing things of which men and women are fully capable, but just don't do in the world I had known, without the doer being considered "criminal" or "deranged." Here the same things are obviously considered highly moral. There seems to be a total reversal of values.

There is no government and there are no laws here. There are formal agreements between people here whose protection I can expect when and if I join in the agreements. But until then I could be killed by anyone and no law would be broken. Translated into values that are familiar to me, my status here is that of an enemy alien. If I had seen enough to have dangerous "spy" information, I might be killed. This I learned after I had thoroughly convinced Kirk that I did *not* want to have him return me to San Francisco.

But let me put things in order. Very carefully Kirk filled the scales with piece after piece of information and let me weigh each piece against my decision to stay. He let me look at each piece fully and re-weigh the total each time before he added another. If there was going to be a breaking point he wanted to know exactly where it was.

First he wanted to know if I would prefer to go back to San Francisco if he went with me and we were able to get our old jobs back or ones similar to them.

I told him that I would not because I thought he was happier here and I thought I could probably learn to be happier here. I could see his great relief that we had made the first hurdle. He said that brought us to an honest basis: The first had been only a hypothetical question which he had hated to ask. He then made it clear to me that he would not at all have considered staying in San Francisco with me.

He realized that such an attitude of his, when known to me, was the first weight against my staying that he was putting in the scale. He gave me time to consider it.

I considered it as a reality — not a principle — and accepted it. He was satisfied with that.

Then he asked me another which he told me in advance was a hypothetical question. Which place would I choose on the basis of my knowledge if he were in neither?

I could not be sure then and I cannot be sure now. I told him then that I thought I would choose to go back. Now my curiosity is so greatly aroused that I think I would choose to stay here. But at the time it was enough for him that I didn't feel *strongly* against being here without him.

Then he made it very strong that a contract between a man and woman for reciprocal sexual fidelity would have no support here. Also he told me that the general attitude here is that any such private agreement is imprudent and against good taste. He wanted no implication that such an agreement exists between us.

Although it would break my heart to have our relations other than exclusive of all others I agreed that I want no contract spoken or implied. This is true. I want to hold him if I do because he wants me.

And then we came to the place where he thought he might be weighting the scales with more than I could take. I could see the hours of lonely thought he had given the problem of how to make himself understood to me — to some zombi who had not absorbed understanding of what he had to say with her mother's breast milk, and had it articulated to her reason as soon as she could talk and think. Hours! He had given a lot more thought to it than hours. He had given days, months, years. All his life he had been thinking how he could tell of it to someone in the outside world. And now the moment had come.

"You have probably believed ever since you were taught it as a baby," he said, "that words are harmless, that freedom of speech always gravitates toward truth, goodness, and beauty. I don't hold that viewpoint but to try to convince you *by words* that words are not always the tools of reason would be to make my own words suspect. I'm not a fool and so I'm not going to do that. But I do have to say something against what I know you have been taught to believe, and right now there is only time to say it in words. I'm not trying to convince by the use of words; I'm just stating my position.

"In the world you come from it appears to me that language is used to control and destroy the integrity, the wholeness, of individual zombis; as sex odors are used to control and destroy the integrity, the wholeness, of individual bees in a beehive. One could say that the functioning hive is an accomplished reality and so it is truth. One could say that the smooth intricate working of the hive is beautiful. One could say that the resultant harmony is good. The discussions of such a subject could be endless. I am an individual man who sees the outside world's cultural tendency to make integrated individuals into components of a group as following the same pattern that once was followed when the beehive was evolved. I don't accept it as good for myself. In self-defense I must oppose it in others. I call that self-defense because, while they cannot impose their ideas on me, they can deprive me of an unconditioned mate and can take from me my children and condition them. They throw masses of people against dissenting individuals.

"Here we have a few people who think as I do. We are so few that we take up a space about as big as a pencil dot on a big scale map. We are consciously creating a way of life that moves in a direction diametrically opposed to that which the bees once followed and which most of the people of the world have been following for at least the ten thousand years of recorded history.

"We have been isolated only a few generations but already we are tending to become dangerously ignorant of how to deal with the opposing trends that threaten us a very short distance away. We need to keep bringing in fresh knowledge of the outside world. But we also need to assimilate and become immune to that knowledge. Otherwise we will be overrun and destroyed by it. We have to take it in little doses.

"I think we can take much more than we are getting and have a healthy growth from it. My father thought so. He brought in four persons, two men and two women, that he thought would fit in. Three of the four turned out to be unassimilable. They couldn't be sent back to reveal the fact of our existence to those who would destroy us. He felt responsible for bringing them here so he killed them. He risked his own life three times to do so. He is dead now. His death is not directly related to his act of killing them.

'He did nothing that is here considered 'illegal' or wrong. However he is often pointed out in retrospect as one who showed very poor judgment."

Kirk told me this as a simple statement of facts. There was no apology. I suspect that if any emotion had crept into his voice it would have been pride that his father had done the honorable thing.

"One of the women," he continued, "turned out all right. The incident left some doubt about the wisdom of bringing anyone in, and about the complete trustworthiness of the remaining woman.

However, she is now almost fully accepted. She was one of your hostesses at your luncheon table the day we worked in the fields. I like her.

"Partly to help her and partly to help my father's memory, but mostly because I, myself, believed in it, I wanted to show that my father's idea was good; that he simply made a bad choice in three of the four persons, and that he made a mistake in trying to bring in more than one at a time. I went to the University of California looking for some *one* person to bring in, but I gave up the search.

"Then I went to work as a truck driver to absorb more knowledge of the zombi world for myself. You know what happened then. I met you and decided you could safely be brought in, that you were the finest person I had ever known, and that I wanted you with me.

"I think that you are good for me and for the people here, and I think that the people here are good for you. I can't believe that there will ever be trouble. But I want you to know my attitude. If I take you back now, no one would believe there is such a place as this, and everyone would believe you were crazy if you said so. I think it would be bad for you and bad for me, but if you want it I'll do it.

"If I don't take you back now, tonight, I won't take you. The thing that maybe will frighten you is that I'll feel responsible for protecting everyone here from anything I think you are doing that harms them. After you know more I wouldn't let you leave for many years, if ever, and I wouldn't tolerate certain things that you might conceivably insist were harmless and part of your essential right to freedom of speech. There's no law here against these things that you might do or say. I brought you here and I alone would take the full responsibility of being your judge, jury, and, if necessary, your executioner."

I, of course, have condensed Kirk's words and made them blunter than they were. Also I have turned into a little speech what was a long conversation. But that is the substance of it as I heard it. We discussed it at great length. I think I understood him perfectly. And I chose to stay on those conditions.

Of course, Kirk believed from the first that I would or he would never have brought me here. But he knew from the first, as I know now, that I would no more have come with him in the beginning if I had heard this all in words than I would have taken off with him in a backyard rocket for a colony of blue angels on the moon. So he has had long lonely doubts since the first moment he knew we could become important to each other.

During all those days when I thought he was simply someone with an undeserved criminal record, or an alien in San Francisco illegally, who could not trust his secret to me, I knew he needed someone terribly, and I wanted to be that someone. I now see that the need was even greater than I had imagined it and, because I first had to develop my knowledge and understanding, I would have been totally unable to help. Even here he has been acting entirely alone among hundreds of people who were mostly unsympathetic or even hostile to what he was doing, who could not forget some similarity to things done by his father.

When I realized fully what our relationship has really been, I wanted to do more than relieve him of my weight. I wanted to give back to him in full measure all the vital energy that his lonely carrying of me had drained from his being. I had been too heavy for him to carry the full month. He was taking his supporting arms from around me, setting me down before he had planned, and I wanted to show him that I not only could stand and walk by myself but could reach out my hand to him as a comrade. In someway I let him know that. I know he knew it. I could feel a joy well up and fill his being until it overflowed at the touch of him. Suddenly I knew that a strong man's need for love is greater than that of a sniveling weakling in the same proportion that his strength, dignity, and commitment to honor are greater. With this knowledge a whole new vista of my value as a woman opened up before me. And, as I realized that I could find in myself the capacity to satisfy so great a need as Kirk's, I felt a bond being welded between us of such strength that its very memory will keep me forever from the fear of loneliness.

How close are pain and joy and ecstasy, and the throb of loneliness made whole. How terrible and wonderful when it all comes into the focus of one little moment — one long delicious instantaneous eternity. So much seems packed into so little when the purposeful yearning of millions of generations, whose past is dammed up in two separate bodies, grasp a single moment to cry "yes" to all time and all creation. Last night our bodies sought to pledge as a link in eternity what our reason refused to insult our beings by pledging in words. I feel as sure that the link was established as if I had already felt new life stirring in me.

10.

For several days I haven't had time nor felt in the mood to write. New knowledge has come so fast that writing could never catch up and I had thought that the urge to write was gone. Certainly some of the half understood impulses that prompted me have dissolved or become unimportant. But I think I will keep on awhile. There will probably be others like me brought in someday and I would like to be able to look back and relive my own reactions.

I'm glad Kirk didn't wait the full month he had planned before giving me my final choice of going back or, for all time, not relating to the world I had known. But I think I needed every minute of the time he did give me. I still have trouble believing in the reality of the here and now. It looks just like an unfamiliar part of the old zombi world. But it has to be thought about in a different way. Only my knowledge that there are people all around me who see Kirk as sane, when they may have some reservations about me, keeps me from the tendency to think he is a madman telling me wild stories of things that exist only in his imagination. They and their behavior toward me stand as evidence that the relations he talks of as commonplace do exist between people who are not in padded cells or behind bars, who not only are walking about free but are nicer than any I have ever been around. Also it was important for me to learn the daily routine of life here before being confronted with the ideas behind it.

Day to day living is infinitely simpler to understand here than in the world I left. Its simplicity gives it a stronger feeling of reality than the other world has; the other is interlaced with mumbo-jumbo. At the same time the world here gains immeasurably in grace and charm by that simplicity. Just to touch and work with dishes and food and candles and a fireplace and furniture produced by a few knowable persons with no complex skills or tools gives me a new respect for individual ability. I had become overimpressed with spectacular factories and the giant machines of mass production. It takes time for one who has lived under the pressure of millions of people motivated by mass impulses to adjust to the release of that pressure. I guess it is like divers coming up from deep in the sea. They have to go through a process that brings the deep water pressure back to air pressure.

After the relief of finding that he would not have to take me back to San Francisco and leave me, an obligation he had taken alone and unknown upon himself, Kirk also seemed to need a little time for depressurizing. The following morning he went off alone in the woods with a shovel and pickax to open up a creek. He said it had clogged up and was in danger of changing to a course that next winter might flood some trees he particularly wanted to save. Saving a few favorite trees in the middle of miles of forest seemed like a poor excuse for solitude but I was glad to have the day alone.

The next day he offered to take me down and show me some engraved agreements that I would have to sign for the record if I expected the protection of others. In my own mind I was already committed to the new reality I had found. I asked if there were not some planting and gardening we could do that day. It was just a mood. After our day of depressurizing separately, I wanted to be alone with him in some simple little activity that would require no critical thought and no weighty words. I think he invented some work that he had not planned but he seemed happy to do it and we enjoyed the simple work and the warm spring day. We came back to simple moment by moment relations with each other.

We had only postponed for one day going to look at the agreements on which life here is built, but the following morning it was raining. It was cozy by the fireplace after breakfast and I said something about wishing we didn't need to go out.

"We don't," Kirk said. "I thought you might want to see the agreements down at the assembly house. They look impressive set out on a large bronze plaque on the wall. I thought that the impressive appearance might supply the dignity to agreements that you have always associated with laws. But you can look at them here, think about them now, and see them on the wall later."

He went in the next room to get them and I expected him to come back with an elaborate document that it would take hours to read. Instead he came back with a single card and handed it to me.

"This is all you would see if we went down," he told me.

"This is all there is?"

"That's all. Seven items of agreement between individuals. The fifth one limits them from being expanded."

I read the fifth one and reread it, letting its significance sink into my mind: "No additional agreements that give a group's decision effective power over individuals shall be made. Any group of two or more individuals who make other agreements giving a group decision power over individuals, or who fail to abide by these agreements, shall be deemed a conspiracy against individual freedom. All acts against them by an individual or by a group of individuals who have entered into these agreements shall be construed to be self-defense." There was some further explanation added but it did not change anything.

I was afraid to look further. I could not believe that any agreements comprehensive enough to guide all human relations could be limited to the six brief ones I had yet to read. The power of the majority had already been effectively removed by the fifth. Could that possibly mean anything except that one of the other agreements simply delegated dictatorial authority to someone? A dictator having "divine" right by heredity or chosen in some arbitrary manner and then entrusted with absolute authority had to be the answer as I could conceive it. I didn't like it. I didn't like it at all. And for a moment I feared Kirk as a fanatical follower who felt responsible for me and would "if necessary" be my executioner.

With such sudden tenseness of emotion that my eyes blurred, and perhaps my mind blurred also, I read the first agreement. It seemed fairly simple and right. It was an agreement that no man, woman, or child should willfully kill, disable, disfigure, secretly restrain another, or force an offensive sexually-oriented act upon another, and no adult should engage in an offensive sexually-oriented act with a child even with the child's willing consent. Then there was some phrasing that I didn't understand.

The second point I thought I understood as an almost unbelievably strong agreement to prohibit rape. It seemed to call *every* act of procreation rape if *the woman involved* chose to call it that — unless prior to the act, she had given public notice that she accepted the man.

The third, as I understood it, gave everyone full police power, and full power to conduct a public trial for anyone found guilty of violating any of the agreements.

The fourth made it clear that no one was required to give testimony at a trial but specifically made perjury subject to the same penalty as other violations of the agreements.

The sixth agreement was more complicated. It used the word "sovereign" which I already knew I didn't understand. The word was used in connection with "formal combat" and my first impression of the whole sixth point of agreement was vague.

The seventh made death within twenty-four hours the invariable penalty for breaking any agreement.

There were no further agreements. The whole was inconceivable. I could not visualize how those agreements could replace the whole body of law by which people usually seek to govern themselves fairly. There were some definitions clarifying two categories of people, "sovereign" and "shielded," and the concept of the categories was part of the agreements. I would have to re-read with these definitions in mind to get the full sense, but I could not believe what I had glimpsed.

I was glad we had not gone down to look first at the agreements on the assembly wall. It would have been embarrassing for me to let anyone but Kirk see my expression of uncomprehending blankness.

"No property laws?" I protested against the vacuity at which I was looking. "No provisions for raising taxes and electing administrators? Nothing about public works or schools? You are civilized and educated and so is everyone I have met here. I've seen no bands of hoodlums and I've seen nothing that I would call crimes but I don't think this is a race of angels that has been bred up. The people here are nice but they seem to be just ordinary people, and I know ordinary people are fully capable of selfish, overbearing behavior. I've seen a few people here that I wouldn't trust very far. I can see things in their faces. I understand them because I have the same things in me and I know how they feel. I have less violence in me than a lot of people I've seen here and I *know* I couldn't be depended on to be an angel in a world without laws."

"What might you do?"

"I . . . I . . . . . . Well, I don't think everyone here can be as happy as I am. If I were hungry or cold or in need I'm sure I'd be capable of stealing."

"If you were hungry, or cold or in need I'm sure no one here would object to your taking what you wanted with or without knowledge of the person who had it."

I hit the ceiling and I know my voice showed my anger. "You are no goody-goody Buddha-like all-humanity-loving, tender-hearted screwball. And I suspect no one here is. When you said the other night you would kill me, if necessary, I believed you literally. I still believe you are entirely capable of doing it."

Kirk was maddeningly calm. He has now told me that he has entirely Northern European heritage but his calmness was an awful lot like what I might have expected from Ghengis Khan. "That's all that's necessary," he said. "If everyone feels that everyone else is capable of anything, not excluding killing him, it keeps each one from offending against the other. Here everyone not only is

53

capable and has a free hand but feels obligated to act against what he considers improper conduct."

"And if someone's idea of improper conduct is not as improper as his act against it?"

"Then someone else acts until an acceptable state is reached. The thing is that each individual case requires *individual* action and individuals each feel obligated to do something. All are free to act *individually*. Any *group* action not included in the agreements begins to crowd the fifth point of those agreements. A potential dictator can be stopped when he gets his first followers. But perhaps more significant, no majority can make laws to be pressured on dissenting individuals by group force."

Kirk's "oriental" calmness was really just an honesty that would not try to distort reason by injecting emotional pressure into his words. He did not want to convince me by his words. He just wanted to tell me as clearly as possible what I wanted to know.

He asked me to imagine any possible thing I might do to offend others and he would explain how it could be dealt with under the agreements.

In my imagination I became a succession of hardened or petty criminals. Having been brought up with television I was pretty good at it. Kirk told me how he would deal with me. As happens on TV I became interested in the game just as a game and when I realized it I was a little ashamed of myself. However I committed so many crimes and was dealt with in so many surprising and effective ways that I began to respect those seven points of agreement. The respect had to be for the agreements and the people who chose to live by them; in our scenario there was no array of futuristic electronic marvels used by superbly clever detectives — with the comically incompetent aid of one or two dumb cops to give the inhuman system a human touch. Finally I began to see that I was looking at a simple pattern of conduct agreed upon by people relying on nothing more — nor less — than their innate intelligence. And I began to organize the agreements in my own mind. The way I organized them for myself is a little different from the order in which they are written.

First comes the matter of word definitions. Instead of using the words adult and minor, female and male, authority and layman, and the many other pairs used outside to designate *and confuse* social roles, these agreements use only two words, sovereign and shielded. Everyone who commits oneself to this way of life is either "sovereign" or "shielded." Anyone who has "reached the age capable of procreation" may become sovereign simply by putting up a public notice to that effect. A child is born under the shield of the mother, or under the shield of her sovereign if she is shielded. "Shielded" means a private agreement, publicly posted, whereby a sovereign must be removed before the shielded can be required to engage in formal combat. A sovereign has more prerogatives and also more responsibilities. The relationship between sovereign and shielded can ordinarily be revoked by a notice posted by either. However if the relationship is entered into as a compromise in the course of combat it is permanent and irrevokable.

A sovereign can challenge another sovereign to formal combat. This might be called a duel but it is no braggadocio public display of courage or skill. This "formal combat" has its conditions clearly spelled out. There is little chance for playing to the grandstand. The combatants hunt and find each other in a circumscribed area and there are no rules within the area and no observers. The only weapons agreed upon are a knife of specified maximum blade (metric measurements are used but blade is about 10 inches) and a specified length of cordage (about 50 feet). The combat area is big and the idea is to permit an intelligent but weaker man to use his intelligence. The conditions are so set as to reduce the weight of brute force or a single learned skill to a point where the whole man is in the contest. There is also an opportunity to work out misunderstandings. A three day waiting period between challenge and combat is specified. There is no limit to how often a man can challenge but one man cannot be challenged and fought more than once a year.

The ever present possibility of formal combat pressures every sovereign to seek reciprocal respect and good relationship with every other. Disregard of other's wishes is not something to be done lightly. The shielded know that if they disregard the wishes of their one sovereign he will simply remove his shield and they will be under the discipline of all sovereigns.

Everyone, shielded or sovereign, has full police power. Anyone can give notice and conduct a trial three days after the notice. However only sovereigns have a vote at the trial. Majority vote determines guilt but only these offenses are subject to public trial:

(1) Willfully killing, disabling, or disfiguring another, except in formal combat, self-defense, or enforcement of the agreements; forcing an offensive sexually-oriented act upon anyone, or engaging in such an act with a child even though no force is used; secretly

restraining another.

(2) Leaving the community or refusing combat after a challenge.

(3) Perjury at a trial (testimony is not mandatory).

(4) Rape, defined as any act of procreation that a woman chooses to call rape if she has not made a public acceptance of the man.

This new concept of rape will take some getting used to. Apparently this crowds out the concept of marriage. By posting a public notice a woman formally accepts a man as her sexual partner. If there has been no such acceptance he is subject to conviction for rape if the woman brings charges against him anytime within three months after the act. The woman's disapproval of the act, and the weight of testimony verifying that the act took place, are all that are needed to condemn him for rape. No consideration is given to the possibility that a woman accepted a man on her own free will at the time and later changed her mind. She even has three months to make up her mind. A woman can be a very dangerous person here.

In practice a woman is usually shielded. Children are usually shielded by their father. The man whom a woman accepts as her lover usually becomes her sovereign, but the two acts are independent of each other. Any implication of bargaining for a shield or bargaining for a woman's acceptance, that is, making the separate relationships into a contractual obligation, would be looked upon as shameful. For a man to bargain for a woman's acceptance would be like bargaining for a whore. For a woman to bargain for a sovereign's shield would be to admit that she did not inspire protection for herself alone. Some women feel a point of pride that causes them to be sovereign. (Inger's mother was sovereign all her life.) Some women who were involuntarily sovereign have acquired a permanent shield by challenging a man and then playing on his reluctance to kill them when in the combat area. Even forceful rape is not defined as rape in the combat field, but no acceptance of a man is implied because the man becomes a woman's permanent sovereign as a result of a challenge. The status has to be announced by both before they are permitted to leave the combat field. There are all sorts of real cases on record and I plan to go down and study them over at great length some time.

Kirk says there are also records of all trials for about seventy years. I want to dig through them sometime too. This urge to make my evaluation of the agreements by studying the historical action makes me feel a little ashamed. I think I should be able to project ideas of my own and choose between them on some reasoned basis. I should not see the choice as already hopelessly overweighted by available evidence. But I realize now that I cannot. I could never have made a purely intellectual choice between the way of life here and the one I had lived under.

Kirk is carrying me still. He has given me a new reality after I chose to cut myself off from the old, and said choose this reality or choose to create your own. I find nothing against his reality and much that I can say in its favor. I have chosen this but I don't try to fool myself that it was a reasoned choice. I am back to the "whither thou goest I will go" sort of decision.

11.

We talked until noon the day Kirk showed me the little card with the agreements on it. The rain stopped, the sun came out, and in the afternoon we went down to the assembly house. It is another simple one story stone building like the library place, small by San Francisco standards but big for here. I saw the wall with the agreements on the bronze plaque. It is on the inner side of a large assembly room. The room was vacant when we were there. The whole wall opposite the plaque can be opened back so that there is no limit to the number of people who can attend a trial. The portion of the building back of the wall is the main lobby and entrance with record rooms along both sides.

One woman was there. I had met her twice before. Looking after the records and helping anyone who wants to put up a notice is a job people, who don't feel like vigorous activity, rotate at doing. It is done mostly by older women with time on their hands, as charity and church work is done by them in the other world. The woman here was no menial clerk. She came forward to greet us and we addressed ourselves to her as guests meeting their hostess.

I didn't especially like her and we didn't need her help. I would have liked that part of the building to have been empty like the other part. It would have accentuated the feeling I had when we first came in the back way to the empty room with the agreements for this way of life covering one wall — a feeling of unearthing a lost civilization and deciding to make it live again, starting with us. Except for the woman everything seemed deserted, quiet, and impressive in its solitude and unexpected simplicity.

57

One wall of the lobby was a bulletin board with brass frame holders for little cards. All was neat and uncrowded. There were many more blank holders for cards than filled ones; cards are taken down and filed when a month old. The bulletin board was divided into six categories: Shield and Sovereign Changes, Challenges, Lovers, Births, Deaths, and General Notices. I noticed that the space under challenges was vacant.

I filled out and signed a card stating that I chose to live by the agreements engraved on the wall of the building. They were all printed on the opposite side of the card I filled out. This I put in a little frame under General Notices.

Then I filled out and signed a card saying that I accepted Kirk Morgan as my lover and that the act of procreation was not excluded from my concept of desired intimacies between lovers. This I put in another little frame under Lovers.

Kirk and I both signed a card in which he offered me the shield of his sovereignty and I accepted. This he placed in the appropriate frame.

That was all. There was no pomp and ceremony. We were ready to leave. The woman, whose name I don't remember, came around and walked to the door with us. She said that she had believed from the first time she met me that everything would work out well, but she was glad to see it was all settled. I bowed, then straightened and held out both my hands to her. She bowed then reached out both her hands and touched my finger tips. Kirk and she went through the same ritual. It is used here both for a formal greeting and a formal leave taking. She closed the door behind us leaving us alone in a clearing in the woods with nothing to do but go home.

Suddenly I felt in my bones something I had always known only in words before — the reason why church and state have so often triumphed over reasonable individuals. Popes and Caesars know that bread and reason are not enough. People want bread and circuses. And I was one of the people — the vulgar populace. I felt cheated. I was fully aware that I had already been living with Kirk for a month but if I had been back in the old world and we planned to stay together there would have been a marriage ceremony. Maybe under the circumstances I wouldn't have felt like a long white veil and orange blossoms but there would have been something. Here I had gone through something as important as becoming a citizen and getting married — doing both in fifteen minutes by simply putting up my own little notices in the presence of one incidental and not particularly welcome witness. I was angry at all the people here.

When the door was closed behind us I turned to Kirk and found him a thousand miles away from me, absorbed in some thoughts of his own. I ran at him and beat on his chest with my fists. I was not making a cute zombi feminine gesture; I wanted to hurt. "You people here are fools," I screamed between my teeth. "Fools! Insensitive fools!"

He looked at me uncomprehendingly and I almost broke into hysterical tears as I stopped beating on him and ran into his arms. After a moment I got hold of myself and laughed. He took my shoulders in his hands, balanced me on my own feet, and looked at me.

"This is a big occasion for me," I said, wiping away the tears that had seeped through. "I feel that I have done something important. There should be some sort of ceremony."

"What would you like?" he asked. I didn't know whether he thought I was being silly and wanted to ridicule me by facing me with a blank wall, or whether he was taking me seriously.

"I have just said I accept the world here," I told him. "I made a decision and posted it for everyone to see. Somebody should beat drums."

I laughed at my foolishness and he joined me. We were together again.

He gave me a hand up on my horse, mounted himself, and as we started off side by side at a slow trot, he said, "Everybody gave you a welcoming party when you came. Can't you just think of your card as a thank you note — one that leaves no doubt of your sincerity?"

I thought about it and was impressed that he was right. I thought about it some more and was very much impressed. I said so.

"But what about my accepting you to exclusion of all else?" I asked. "Here a contractual marriage would be shameful and kept secret. In the other world a notice like I have just put up would be something shameful to be kept secret. I really feel very happy to be in a world where I can put it up and I put it up there proudly. But that little card is too inconspicuous. I want to shout it out loud. I want everybody to know and I want to know they know."

"Would you like to give a big party and tell everybody?"

"Yes."

"YES," I repeated. "I think I would."

Then I added decisively, "I *know* I would."

He slapped my horse and we broke into a full gallop. "I was right about you," he yelled. "You're tops. You see things as they are. Go ahead. Have a party."

"You mean it?"

"Sure I mean it."

We got home with our horses in a white lather. We had raced recklessly and the ride did me a lot of good.

12.

Well, I gave a party but I'm not very proud of the way I did it. I had all the help I could use from individuals but I had no familiar conventions to guide me and I must face the fact that I still have a zombi dependence on them.

. . . There is a therapeutic value to this writing — like Catholics going to confession or neurotics going to psychiatrists. My confession today is an admission to myself that I am no longer proud of being one of the vulgar populace who look to their Caesars for bread and circuses. I *am* still one of them but I am ashamed of it. I can only hope that, knowing how completely I have been only a dot in a circus audience, my horror at seeing myself as a faceless, formless, gray shadow may cause me to question more closely what I would be if set apart and looked at by myself.

The other day in the store I half consciously defended myself from Bingee's viewpoint by thinking of her as an adolescent pretending a sophistication she didn't have. I didn't want to look closely at what I was seeing because it made me feel inferior. Now I must admit that she, and all the rest of the people here, have something that a Caesar doesn't even have the vision to aspire to. And where does that leave the populus vulgarus? Where does it leave me?

I don't even know how to describe what it is in the people here that makes me, and others in the world I came from, their inferiors. Looking at them from the common viewpoint of the world I left they are a bunch of dirt farmers with a mania for individual independence. Measuring them by an anthropologist's scale of values they would unquestionably be a people of even lower development than those of some little midwest provincial town, and completely out of the field of comparison to the people of San Francisco. But somewhere down deep in me I know the standards are all wrong. This is a higher civilization. It is so much higher that I only get a glimpse of its superior qualities — a very fleeting glimpse — when standing on tiptoe.

There is absolutely nothing different about the people here that I can get my teeth into. They are simply more alive and more conscious of what they are doing. The thing that throws me is my habit of thinking that a superior people would have intricate and marvelously impressive new gadgets. Here everyone looks at the natural world and really sees it for the marvel it is — and seeing, has no desire to overlay it with a world of manufactured articles. I suspect that all anthropologists are fools and the highest civilizations are those that left no trace. There is something wrong with a people who have to build a city and an electronic computer to impress themselves because they have exhausted their interest in a seashell and a worm. The same unfeeling dependence on circuses requires a microscope and laboratory techniques in a ceremonious atmosphere before they will look again at the seashell and the worm.

With all its more mechanically refined and more glittering ceremonies, the world I came from is somehow inferior to the less impressive world here. I think the difference may be in the greater sparsity of conventions here. The absence of guidelines for every move makes everyone think more creatively. And I now realize *fully* something of vast importance: Crude creations are greater than exquisite imitations.

My trouble was that I was looking for something to imitate and, when I did not make the most of my opportunity as a production director, my party was saved from insipidity only by the kindness of others.

I found that acceptance parties are not at all unusual. There are even a lot of commonplace ways of giving them, ways that have sprung up by repetition. But here they lose value by repetition instead of becoming honored traditions. Definitely they are not conventions in the sense that one feels obligated to follow them. Conventions are of the most basic nature possible and better ways of doing the basic things are looked for by everyone. Anything goes. But anything that is done is watched for meaningfulness. Everything — *everything* — one does is looked upon as articulation of one's being. Silence, failure to do things, is articulation. Of course this is true everywhere but here everyone is intensely conscious of it.

After discussing with Kirk where I could have a party and how to invite people, I found that I could simply claim the hall where the welcoming party had been held for me. He suggested that I give the word to Inger, Bingee, and Lolena and let them take care of spreading invitations. Since I was going to announce something already posted he said I should do it before it was too old and suggested two nights later.

The next morning — after one night had already gone — he offered to ride by and tell the girls. As he left he said he wouldn't be back. He was gone before I realized that since I was going to make a public display of choosing a lover he, of course, couldn't participate. But when I first saw that he had dropped everything in my hands I almost panicked. If he hadn't left so soon I would have called off the whole thing. I broke two of my beautiful blue dishes that morning and seemed unable to find anything I looked for.

But before I had time to despair completely, I heard what sounded like a rescuing cavalry coming up at full gallop. I ran to the door and found the three girls descending on me full of enthusiasm, encouragement, and offers of assistance. Kirk had told them what I wanted to do and they all approved wholeheartedly. They said I was to consider them completely at my disposal until I opened the door to receive the following night.

I had seen these girls' imperious teamwork in running a rough plowing operation involving horses and men in the field; their behavior at that time was the reverse of a preparation for their way of offering me their help. They completely gave themselves into my hands with an attitude of "I am yours, command me."

Help of course I needed but what I needed more was a pattern of action. I asked for ideas and precedents and I got them in such profusion and variety that it was like having none at all. The range of precedents sounded so great that at one end I am sure priests could have picked up some ideas for adding solemnity to a high mass, and the other end would have made an artists' and models' ball look staid and puritanical. I tried to get a datum point by asking what I should wear and showed them the clothes I had brought with me.

Already I had made a tentative decision but I didn't even get a chance to try anything on and show how I looked in it. They ran through my clothes mostly without taking them off the rack. Inger, who is about my size and also blond, showed some interest in one or two things that she said she would like to see me wear *sometime* but I suspected that the three were unanimous in the opinion that nothing I had could be used for the occasion. I asked for suggestions.

"You need something that shows *you*," Bingee said, and explained that she thought it should have no detracting cut or color.

Between them they came up with ideas so fast that I almost got lost, but among the colors suggested, I showed a preference for rust. They picked up the first positive thing I had said and suggested a forest motif for decorating the hall to make me stand out.

I said rust and a forest green background sounded good to me. Immediately Inger, who had at first suggested that I wear green, did a quick about switch. She said she had at least three hides of a wonderful rust that all matched and, *if I would let her,* she would ride over and get them for me to see, and be back before we were well started planning the hall.

I was doubly confused. I was confused by her asking my permission, and by her mention of *hides* for my clothes. While trying to decide which incongruous thing to take up first, I guess I stared at her blankly.

"May I?" she repeated her request for my permission.

"Of course," I said. I tried to smile but I don't know whether or not it was really a smile that came out.

She was out the door before I could say anything else. Lolena called and asked her to bring some sewing things and, from her horse, already in motion, she yelled back that she would. It had all happened so fast that I hadn't got over the shock that they could be talking about my wearing leather. I remembered seeing no leather at the welcoming party for me. I turned to Lolena and Bingee and asked if they really thought I should wear leather clothes.

"Oh, I know why you are disturbed," Bingee laughed. "You remember those things we had on in the field the other day. We can make you look better than that."

They had been talking of a short sleeveless sheath. It didn't sound *too* bad in leather and as they were obviously waiting for me to make a decision, I said, "O.K. A rust sheath it is," and felt like I had taken off on a steep ski run.

"Now how about your shoes?" Bingee asked. "Do you have anything that might be right?"

"With a leather sheath! I doubt it. You and Lolena look." I brought out what I had with me. The selection was very meager. Bingee dived for my ballet slippers.

Lolena turned to me with a vision of wonder written in her

eyes. "Can you dance — alone?" she asked.

I have had several years of ballet and have dreamed of myself alone in a spotlight but I have never even been in a real performance. I saw what was in Lolena's eyes and thought it fantastic. I told her I could dance fairly well but certainly I couldn't be the star.

"I have watched you move," Bingee grew excited. "I know you could do it."

I was confused as to what they had in mind and said so. They said my ballet slippers should be dyed to make me look barefoot, went into details of the forest decorations for the hall, and talked of music, lights, and everything as if I were a professional dancer. I protested that I wouldn't think of trying to dance tomorrow night without preparation and rehearsal.

"That's no problem," Lolena was becoming enthusiastic. "You can choose the music and the orchestra can play what you want. They have endless selections they can play without rehearsal."

"And if they feel your mood," Bingee added, "and start improvising for you, it will be better. Don't you feel it already?" She began to dance and kept on talking. "You are alone on the floor and the hall is full of handsome men. You are to choose one. They hold out their hands to you." Lolena held out her hands as Bingee danced up to her. "They try to grab and hold you." Lolena came into the dance executing movements of attempting to take while Bingee repulsed her and looked for someone who wasn't there. I began to understand and tried to join in. Lolena forced me to change roles by dancing an attempt to hold me, to pull me back. Bingee came then to try to take me and I took on the seeking, sought-after solo part.

They continued the part of trying to catch me, beginning to sing wordless music that I responded to as best I could, then they clapped their hands in approval.

"See. You can do it," Bingee exclaimed.

"You are good," Lolena smiled happily. "You could carry it off grandly and you'd be lovely."

"But I'm not choosing a lover," I protested. "He's already chosen. The notice has been posted."

"That's all right," Lolena assured me. "Everyone understands. You are announcing the choice."

While my head was still spinning with the idea that I was mad to even think of such things, Inger came back with a bundle. She spread the skins out and we crowded around to look. Leather didn't seem like such a wild thought when I saw how soft they were.

"Doeskin," Inger told me. "Will they fit your plans? How are they going?"

Bingee asked enthusiastically if she could tell Inger. I had never before been in a position of what seemed such absolute command of people and their asking permission of me continually surprised me. I said she could. She brought out my ballet shoes, said I could dance, described her idea of my short sheath, gave a brief description of the choreography, talked of the forest motif for decorating the hall and said that was as far as we had gone. "How does it sound?" she asked. "I know we were using some of the ideas you had planned for *your* acceptance party but I knew you wouldn't mind. You have said you weren't going to choose a lover for a long time yet."

Inger was silent and thoughtful for a moment. I was framing words to protest my ignorance of what I had done, without dodging my responsibility for moving in on her plans, when she started talking more slowly and deliberately than was her habit.

"I don't think it's quite right," she said. "For me, yes. But not for Valerie. I thought you had all seen the difference when you thought my suggestion of green would be the wrong color. I thought my changing to rust was agreeing with you."

I didn't understand and was silent. Bingee and Lolena also waited.

Inger looked at me with a troubled brow and said, "Valerie, I was born here. I'm of the forest. I would wear green to say so. Then I would do a solo ballet to show my — well, aloofness — no one would try to dance with me. Men would reach for me but no more. Then I would choose. I don't know where it would go from there because I don't yet know who will be my lover but I would bring him away from the others in some way that would accent my uniqueness and his."

I was listening carefully now and when she stopped I urged her to go on. She continued with the same concentration on trying to communicate.

"One gives a party to say something to everyone there. In this case you are announcing your choice of Kirk as your lover. Everyone knows he brought you here from zombiland. There may still be some question in a lot of minds as to whether you belong. The color acknowledges your conspicuousness in the forest, but the material claims your basic identity with the wild and your acceptance of it. I think you need to emphasize that acceptance, and a ballet would estrange you as much as if you wore one of those dresses you brought with you. I plan for my father to announce my party and receive the guests and I appear later. But I think that you should receive your guests and dance with all of them, simple ball-room dancing, unless you really want to set yourself apart, as I do. But in your case it wouldn't ring true after your notice accepting the way of life here that you posted only yesterday. It would be saying that it was a half-hearted acceptance."

I was horrified at what I might have done and said so. There were no rigid conventions, but one was expected to have artistic judgment.

Bingee and Lolena admitted Inger was right and said that we must go slower and give me time to think if they were going to be any real help. "*You* must direct *us*," they said.

I, who was supposed to be leading, had experienced only a brief flight of imagination as I had followed the girls when their enthusiasm caused them to race on ahead. Now, scared by the vista of total freedom they had shown me, I drew back into my little zombi shell of remembered conventions, dragging with me the hints of similarities I had glimpsed. Inger's statement that she had planned for her father to announce her party had struck a chord that was familiar to me. I remembered the tall dignified man with white hair and a scar on his face at my welcoming party and asked if she thought he would help *me* receive guests.

The idea seemed to start a new thought train that all of them were less enthusiastic about but they said they felt sure Dag would do it and suggested that I might want to ask Margaret to help me receive too.

I jumped at the idea so quickly I couldn't gracefully back out when I remembered what Kirk had told me about Margaret. She was one of the four people his father brought here from the outside and then killed the other three.

When he had told me that she was one of the hostesses at my luncheon table that day we worked in the fields, I remembered her immediately because I had already developed a strong liking for her. She had seemed to reciprocate my interest in her that day but had given no indication of the bond between us, if it can be called that — the fact that we both came from zombiland and even both from UC Berkeley.

I don't quite know why but I thought her background would make it wrong to have her receive with me. I guess I had some vague idea that I would be flaunting an alliance with the enemy. However once started I let the plan develop and I had no cause to regret it. She, who has three children "by three different fathers" as she told me at the luncheon, has now accepted Dag as her lover. He is her sovereign, the sovereign of her children, and the sovereign of Inger, Lolena and Bingee. Inger is his daughter. They all live together in one big log house, and the attitude of people here toward them seems to be that they constitute a pillar of stability.

Margaret came around and talked to me about the party when we were decorating the hall but there were too many people around for any suggestion that we had confidences to share. I like her enormously. She is probably not over thirty-five, her figure is still very good and her face — clear skin, brown hair and brown eyes — is pretty, almost beautiful. An enormous love of life shows through her face. She doesn't exactly seem young but I feel that there is no barrier of ages between us. She often meets my eyes with interest and I would like to share confidences with her on equal terms but while we were decorating the hall and while she was receiving with me there was no opportunity to become intimate. Someday I want to make an opportunity.

But to get back to where I was. I had seen something I recognized and I latched on to it in typical zombi fashion. I gave myself into the hands of the three girls as far as my clothes were concerned and told them that I simply wanted to have a party to announce my acceptance of Kirk in a way that would also express my thanks for the way I had been received here. They took up where we left off in good spirits.

Bingee drew a sketch, they consulted over it, asked me to decide on disputed details, then, without pattern, they began to cut and sew.

From that time until the party they literally never left me except to do errands on my behalf. They turned me out with such subtly flattering simplicity that when I looked in the mirror I couldn't believe I was I. Lolena, seeing my expression as I looked at myself, said wonderingly, "I believe you've never really seen yourself before. Didn't you know you are beautiful?" A lump tied up in my throat that was hard to swallow at such a compliment from someone whose mirror could never leave her the slightest doubt of her beauty.

Eight or ten men and women showed up to help decorate the hall but my three loyal aides saw to every sprig of tree and flower, the location of every chair, the intensity of every light and the precise directions its beams would fall. Most important of all they sensed my frightened dependence on them and, without appearing to be instructing me, they talked about the way things had gone at other parties until they had given me several examples for everything I wanted to do. Because of this I felt utterly confident, fully at ease, and gloriously happy when at last I stood at the door receiving my guests.

I had learned in the past two days that everyone was intensely conscious of clothes and my interest in what people were wearing was at a high pitch. When Dag and Margaret arrived to help me receive I was a little surprised at the way they were dressed. I don't know what I expected and I can't go back and dig up my past thoughts now. Dag was wearing brown leather trousers and beautiful boots of simple lines made from the same material. He wore a cloth shirt of almost matching brown but a little lighter. The cut and color of this gave a suggestion of military lines, particularly the cut of the collar and shoulders. But the texture spoke against the military effect. The cloth seemed to be homespun and hand loomed. He wore a wide leather belt and a short sword or knife at the left side. I especially noted the knife and decided the blade was within the length specified in the agreements.

Margaret wore a dress of cloth that also seemed to be homespun and hand loomed but was of a finer thread and weave. It was a darker brown than Dag's, almost black. The lines were very clean, giving a simple dignity. There was a slight accent, a thin rolled facing where the dress joined in front, but it was very faint and was much less noticable than a silver pin she wore on her left breast. The pin was a replica of Dag's short sword, pinned on horizontally and had Dag's name, "Angskuld," lettered on it in gold.

After the guests began to arrive they continued to come with very little break in their crowding in. I was trying to remember everyone I had met before, trying to see what the new ones were like, and then I was keyed up to a heightened interest in clothes and looked for expressions of feeling in everything I saw.

Many of the men wore leather, various colors, usually on the dull side; some wore all leather, some cloth shirts; but I noticed no one but Dag who wore a sword. I decided it was the formal mark of a host.

A few of the girls wore leather, usually beaded, but mostly the women and girls wore cloth, plain colored, patterned, with or without jewelry, often elaborate decoration — everything. The variation in dress was enormous. It was like a costume party or a Mardi gras where anything goes. The more I saw the more I could not understand the concern the girls had expressed over the cut, color, and materials of my clothes.

As I stood there bowing and touching fingers with everyone formally I was impressed more and more with the carnival atmosphere and I could hardly restrain myself from grabbing people I had met and liked by both hands or even throwing my arms around them. Although I kept my gestures restrained and formal, my greetings became gradually gayer and more in a carnival spirit.

I looked at the wide difference in dress, emphasized anew by each arriving guest, and wondered how my clothes could have been so important. Several times I thought of my closet full of things that the girls seemed to have dismissed as hopeless and felt that I wouldn't have been out of place in any of them, not even in riding breeches and boots. But when I remember now I know that the girls were right. Each person of that great variety was trying to say something with his clothes. Some were stammering maybe but I was insensitive to even the most articulate. I could only see the total and I wanted to give into the spirit of the party rather than direct it.

It went through my mind that as hostess I was hampering the carnival atmosphere by my formal greetings and I was tempted to give way to it by meeting some guests with drinks instead of bows. Some of the volunteer helpers were circulating drinks freely to the arrived guests and I could hear an atmosphere of gaiety becoming increasingly effervescent.

The girls had left to dress as soon as everything was in order and Dag and Margaret, already dressed, had arrived. I somehow assumed that they would wear leather since they thought that I should. Once before they returned I remembered them and felt a little sorry that they might turn up drab amid all the color and gaity. Then I forgot them. When they did come back I was at the same time relieved and surprised. Inger had on a white cloth sheath that came well below her knees but was slit to well above them on the sides. Bingee was wearing a simple white blouse, green skirt and white sandles. She looked like a little girl. Lolena was wearing a tight fitting bodice, long full skirt, all in gay colors, and an enormous amount of jewelry like a gypsy.

They came into the receiving line as if they had not virtually done the whole thing. I was going to follow the impulse I had been bottling up for a long time and hug them but Inger, although smiling in intimate fashion, bowed formally to me and touched my finger tips. "It sounds good," she said, nodding at the laughter and spirited talk going on inside, and without giving me a chance to say anything went on in.

Bingee and Lolena followed Inger's routine and when they had passed, as if it were a signal, Margaret turned to me and said she thought everyone was there and we should not keep them waiting.

Dag held out his hand saying that, inasmuch as Kirk could not be host, he could claim the first dance with me and we should set the example for the evening before everyone became drunk while they were waiting for us.

The floor cleared as we began dancing, leaving us alone, and then slowly couples began to join us on the floor as they would have done outside. I felt the comfortable cotton wool packing of convention closing in around me and I was happy to sink into it. I hadn't seen Kirk since he left me the previous morning after breakfast but whenever I mentioned the fact to anyone they said, "Don't worry. He'll show up when the time comes."

Except for my wonder about when the time would come, I was entirely at ease and enjoying myself very much. Everyone danced or drank and talked as if they were happy to be there and the orchestra was good.

Cutting in on me became increasingly frequent and before long I felt that I'd danced with every man in the house. I began to realize that I had danced with several two or three times. I recognized that familiar partners were turning up more and more frequently and that the factor of eligibility, as the word would have been used in zombiland, seemed to be constantly going up. I'd noticed the day of the field work that men seemed to be very aggressive in their courtship; their compliments to me now were courtship to an extreme that seemed to be pushing the limit. I thought that as a newcomer to the area and as their hostess I should say every complimentary thing I could in return that would not be shamelessly hypocritical. I began to play a game of paying compliment in return for compliment wherever possible.

Everyone stopped dancing long enough to have a drink fairly often and the drinks were fairly strong.

I was beginning to wonder if I could sustain the stepped up ardency in exchanging compliments with the increasingly lively men who were cutting in with increasing frequency. I was getting dizzy with the tempo of rapidly changing partners.

I forgot for a minute that I was hostess and a hostess has the temporary position here that I associated in the outside world only with royalty. Cutting in was so close that we were no longer dancing. Two men pushed each other back from me, each trying to get there first and one said, "I guess you'll have to choose between us." I gave myself to another's arms and said back over my shoulder, "You two fight it out."

That started it. One of them knocked the other down. The one on the floor tripped the other up and they were both sprawling and seeking an advantage. Another man tried to cut in on me, my partner refused to yield, and another fight started. I started dancing with another man and the same thing happened again. It soon became a free for all. Some of the girls seemed to be trying to separate the men fighting and some to be joining in. All were laughing. There were several girls sprawled on the floor. They seemed to be having fun but the whole thing was moving too fast for me and I didn't know whether it was a routine game for such occasions or whether I had made an utter fool of myself.

I began to panic. Then I saw Lolena close by. She was dancing but looking at me with something of a question in her eyes. I ran to her. "Have you seen Kirk?" I cried. We had discussed it and I had planned that, after I had danced with everyone, I would lead Kirk up to the orchestra, have the trumpeter blow a call, and announce that I chose Kirk.

She smiled, a quick smile like an explosive relief of her puzzlement. She stopped her partner and faced me to give emphasis to her words. "In your place I would ask for him," she said. She smiled at me reassuringly then went back to her partner's arms and her dancing.

Someone tried to take me in his arms but I pushed him away and looked about helplessly trying to think. I had had several drinks and I was very slow in realizing what I had to do.

At last I ran across the hall between the dancers toward the orchestra looking everywhere for Kirk as I ran. I stopped the orchestra and told the trumpeter to blow a call. He blew until the rafters rang and then there was silence. It was so quiet I could hear my heart beating.

I forgot all the beautiful speech I had thought up. I took a deep breath, smiled, and loudly announced the bare words, "I choose Kirk Morgan. Can anyone tell me where he is?"

"Here!" a chorus came. A dozen men brought a figure in dull green leather toward me from the far corner of the hall on their shoulders, untying thongs from his feet and hands and a gag from his mouth as they came. By the time they were there he was sitting upright on their shoulders like a conquering hero and as they approached he jumped down. They cleared the way and he came toward me.

I rushed into his arms and held on for dear life. He pressed me close for a moment and then "Dance" he said in my ear. "Dance," he called to the orchestra.

The trumpet called loud for attention, the brasses yelled out, the strings cried and sang as if they had been let out of hell for a holiday, then all the instruments joined in a rhythm that swept us up and out on the floor.

The crowd moved back, the scufflers disappeared from the floor, and we danced alone. I cried and laughed at the same time. The relieved frustration of shame and pride at what I had done and what I was doing seemed to be finding escape in every cell of my being. I realize that keeping me from Kirk had only been a little impromptu effort on the part of some of the men to prolong the dance and emphasize that they already knew I had chosen but the little unexpected turn gave a sense of reality that the party would not otherwise have had. It was all that saved it from the dullness of my planning.

I found out later that Kirk had been fully surprised by being held back from my seeing him. At the time we didn't talk but I felt in him an emotional release from the frustration. The music had a compelling rhythm and he danced with great vigor. I was so eager for the movement that I didn't feel his strength as I followed him, just his further reaching at each motion. I imagined we were dancing as I had never danced before — as no one had ever danced before. We danced over the whole world and there was no one in it but us. We danced through days and nights and all eternity.

Gradually I again became aware of the reality around us. No one else was dancing. I remembered that they had all backed to the walls and given us the floor when we started. But the lights seemed dimmer. It was almost dark. My eyes swept the walls.

There were no people! There were no walls even! I felt a little dizzy at the idea and decided I had drunk too much.

We danced on. It didn't really seem to matter that there were no walls. I knew I couldn't hold as much as I had drunk that night but everything was all right. Kirk was there now and his arms were around me.

I alerted myself a little and swept the place where the walls should have been again. The people were all gone, the lights had been dimmed and I could see nothing but the branches of the trees we had used to decorate the hall. It looked as if we were alone out in the woods. It didn't matter, I thought. Then I realized that the orchestra was still playing but the orchestra was not there either. I alerted myself further but the music was still playing and Kirk was still dancing so I kept on dancing.

The feeling of dancing out in the woods alone with Kirk enveloped me and I again gave myself to the mood. I forgot about the orchestra that existed only as sound. Otherwise I felt quite sober and awake; I knew I was really still in the hall and the illusion of forest was created by the decorations we had put up. I wondered a little about the people all leaving but it didn't seem to matter.

Then I had a strong feeling that the forest, the decorations, were moving up on us, closing us in. I became certain that it was literally true. The space in which we were dancing had become smaller and smaller. Now it was very small and not far away from us was the wide entrance door standing open with the night and the starlight outside.

In a flash of understanding I knew and with the knowledge somethig in words went through my mind, " 'till Birman wood do move to Dunsinane." Those trees were moving and my guests were behind them moving them. Except for the orchestra still playing the quietness was absolute. As if we were the only ones in the world, Kirk led me to the door, into the night, and we came home.

I don't regret that I did it. It made me realize how kind everyone here is and how much everyone wants to be helpful. But it also showed me how much accent the lack of rigid conventions puts on everyone's behavior and particularly on the behavior of a hostess. I wish that, as a hostess and as a woman making the most important announcement of her being about the man she loves, I had been a little less of a zombi. I am in a world where it would be as ridiculous to hire a caterer for an acceptance party as it would be to hire a whore for the man one was accepting. If I am going to cease being inferior to the people here, if I am going to rise above Caesars and circus followers, I am first going to have to learn to take over the functions of the Caesars as they affect me.

13.

I always remember Hans Hargrave from the first night when I asked him defiantly, "Am *I* a zombi?" What I saw when he looked directly into my eyes and said that I seemed to be coming awake quite well made me *want* to wake up. I liked him from that

73

moment.

I rode over to the library yesterday morning and he welcomed me as cordially as if he were my grandfather who had been trying to get me to visit him for years.

He is always at the library because he lives there. He has a vegetable garden, some fruit trees, some chickens, and a cow. He admitted with sincere shame that, for the last four years, people have been giving him flour already milled because he has been spending too much time on books to provide his own. Specialization and exchange of services is an utterly unacceptable concept here, although, using this as an example, there are times when it is actually practiced. However every person thinks he must keep direct contact with the source of his biological existence or lose something that should be very much a part of his life as a whole person.

The building that is both his home and a library open to everyone was started three generations ago; Hans is the fourth person who has occupied it most of a lifetime. The library section is open so that anyone can walk in, but it is not public in the sense that a library is public in the outside world; Hans may not be there but everyone recognizes that he is the host and visitors are his guests.

He showed me with pride the additions he had put on and the improvements he had made to the previous structure. His pride was not because it was a lot but because he considered that he had used admirable restraint. He had done no more than what he considered the necessary minimum.

Since I learned that there are no property laws here, my interest in people's undisturbed possession of houses, lands, and animals has been whetted and not completely satisfied. There seems to be no problem. This is an example. This place has a plaque on it expressing the original builder's wish to dedicate it to anyone who would maintain it as a library for the use of all, as it had been used prior to dedication. It had passed through three hands and had been unoccupied for two years when Hans decided to take it over. I asked the same question I have asked several times since I became aware that there are no property laws: "Do people not take things that others have worked for, either take them for their own use or waste them rashly?" In this case I had the vacant building with many books in it as what I considered a prime concrete example.

Hans assured me that, although most of the doors and windows had been nailed shut to keep out birds and animals, no one would have had trouble getting in and no one had bothered the place while it was vacant. Various persons had opened it up, aired and cleaned it, and in the winter had occasionally built a fire in it to keep it dried out, but, so far as he knows, no one took any books that they did not return.

He said that people do occasionally take things that many think they should not. Sometimes men dispute a possessive use of land or buildings, and particularly of streams. Often they fight and sometimes their differences run into formal combat and someone is killed. But not often does it go that far. He admitted that there will doubtless be much more of that sort of thing if and when people take up all the usable land here; but he added that the point where the balance of nature curtails any species with any way of life has to be reached sometime.

My current judgment on this idea — phrased in the language I brought from the outside zombiland that has property laws — is this: Problems arising from what the outside world calls "property" are less here than they are in zombiland, at least for now. Space needed per person is much greater here than outside, so saturation of space by humans can be reached faster here than in the outside world. But *unless mass warfare is the objective* there is no known advantage in having human saturation delayed until everyone is pressed so close that all are irritated by constant awareness of others. This was the opinion Hans expressed, it is Kirk's opinion, and, tentatively, I find it readily acceptable. I will have plenty of time to think about it; saturation is a problem that seems a long way off right now.

While Hans was showing me his place and the simple dignity of his monk-like life, since his "last love" died eight years ago, he told me of his immense enjoyment of my acceptance party. Already, after talking to Kirk and others, the first embarrassment I felt about my remembered behavior had gradually disappeared. Hans helped to remove it still further.

"Your behavior was very revealing of you," he said, in mentioning the party. "I heard you even said to two men, 'You two fight it out.' I hope you can tell me that it is true."

"It is true. But I'm ashamed."

He laughed. "I don't doubt that you're ashamed, but how eloquent. Your shame and confusion and will to go on despite them were eloquently expressed. And the eloquence didn't end with the expression of yourself. Those wonderful fights were a significant portrayal of both the historical development of, and the way back from, the idiocy of state and church authorized marriages. You may not have been fully conscious of what your actions were saying but you were very articulate. I enjoyed your party more than any I have attended in a long time. And acceptance parties can always be looked to with hope for revealing drama. I never miss one."

I told him that I like what I see here but I can't see clearly what is right before my eyes. I went on to say that I chose Kirk while in zombiland and my choice without society's formal authorization seemed formally acceptable here. I told him that by my acts I wanted to voice my approval of a society that could approve what it did not arrogate to itself the prerogative of authorizing, and I recognized that the society spoke back clearly, in announcing its respect for mine and Kirk's privacy, and that I was greatly impressed. Then I got in a conversational lead that I wanted to insert. I said that the full meaning of agreements giving social recognition to the publicly expressed choice of a woman, and giving woman absolute power of life and death over a secret lover, was far from clear to me.

He deliberately passed up my lead.

"It will become clear," he said. "In the outside world there is a group attempt to dictate how things 'should be.' Here there is group recognition and group protection of what the characteristic female temperament contributes to life — just as group approval of formal individual combat is social recognition and group protection of what the characteristic male temperament contributes."

I didn't want to pass up the chance to discuss marriage when I thought I had someone who would relate to it. I pushed a little further. I had already been there a long time but I found everything he said revealed new facets of the general thought patterns here and I wanted to keep him talking. I made the mistake of putting on my most intellectual, my anthropology major, air. I deserved what I got.

"I am beginning to get the impression that monogamy is the most general form of mating here," I said when I could work it in. "I understand that children take the name of either parent or neither. There are no property laws so inheritance has no meaning. But it does seem to me that all this leans towards a matriarchy. I don't object; I'm a woman. But matriarchies which have existed in primitive societies seem to lose out in the competitive race. I am by no means able yet to evaluate what I see here." Maybe I was not

76

quite that bad, but almost.

"Property, nations considered as if they were organic entities, matriarchy, competitive societies — zombi words, zombi concepts," he smiled tolerantly and patted my hand. "You are feeling so sleepy that you start sleep-talking. I have taken you all around, shown you my place, given you a picture of my life, and I have tired you out. Let's have some lunch."

He took me into the kitchen while he continued talking. "I will make you a tea that I brew from native herbs; you will find it refreshes you more than either coffee or the tea you know. I look forward hopefully to the time when we can cease bringing them in. Our importation of coffee, tea and tobacco has gradually dwindled. We could easily do without them if necessary so they would cause no problem if we needed to break all contact with zombiland; but each little thread of interdependence on zombiland, just like interdependence between individuals, is a hazard that might trip us up. We walk a tight rope. We have to be very careful if we are going to have any hope that our way of life can survive the present peak of zombi population and power. . . . But no world beyond what you know here for the moment. Remembering the confused ideas you know from zombiland will always make you sleepy."

I had been there well over an hour and had repeatedly tried to get him to talk about Camp 38 in comparison to the outside world. But he always came back to the here and now. During our morning together I had to be content with comparisons by looking at him, as a representative of the people here, while I, from outside, still had the outside viewpoint.

Hans is slightly built and not much taller than I am. His white hair and amused blue eyes give him the sort of storybook appearance Hollywood would cast as a lovable eccentric making toys for children. As he showed me around his place, a big adjustment in my thinking was needed to realize that he, like almost every other man here, has lived all his life with the calmly accepted knowledge that he would kill another man, not merely in self-defense, but simply because he decided the man needed killing. He would not do it because a jury decided it, or because a congress had declared the man to be a wartime enemy. As an act of his own individual will, he would simply challenge the man to formal combat.

That framework of personal relations here gives such men a new interest for me. It has much more significance to me than if I discovered that such a kindly old scholar was a retired military general.

A nuance in Hans' poise, that I admire, obviously comes from his knowledge that he has never been protected from bigger and cruder men by some intangible thing called "the government." He has always stood ready to protect himself and effectively defy any intrusion on his way of life. The personality nuance is very subtle but fully discernable. He is kind by nature but, in acquired behavior, he is neither ingratiating nor irresponsibly arrogant; he is simple and direct. Although he will not be pushed in a direction he does not want to go, he is still the easiest person to talk with I have ever met. And I suspect that he knows so much that, by comparison, the professors I once respected would be like high school boys.

I'm quite sure that he thinks the outside world is no more than an intellectual junk pile. He said that it contains many mutilated and some solid ideas which he thinks we need to bring in. But he also said that it contains no cohesive ideas that he considers meaningful as an organized whole.

He is a scholar by nature but he obviously has a strong reasoned contempt for those who revere knowledge in the abstract. When I, in school girl fashion, tried to display my learning, he implied that my training in anthropology might have supplied some fragments of knowledge which could be of value to me — but only if I view myself as an innately intelligent person who has grown up in a primitive society. The point he was making was that I must examine the pattern for living that I have known all my life, piece by piece, as if it were not an essential part of me. Although he was always kind, the context of his words made the emphatic point: If I do not I will be entering this world with my thoughts and emotions nothing but a junk pile that will offend everyone here.

I have never met any scholar whose knowledge I respected more. Yet, now that I sit here thinking and writing about him, I suspect there would be no place for him in the outside world. That says something significant about my old zombiland.

We had lunch, a long lunch. Hans was host and waiter. He invited three women and a man who were doing research in the library and they joined us. We talked the whole time about books and education. Education here is radically different from outside. I want to put some of the differences down when I find time. But next time I write I want to go back to the subject of society in relation to the individual, as Hans and I did after the others left.

Right now I want to get outside and enjoy myself. It's a wonderful day.

14.

Writing about my afternoon with Hans is going to tax my ability, I know. But I should get it down before I forget the things he said. Also I want to remember my own attitude, which I know is going to change so much that I will not believe my old self ever existed unless I have it written down.

The others went back to what they were doing; Hans and I had another cup of tea on the terrace. I tried to open the conversation where we left off by asking, "Is society a zombi word?"

He laughed and said, "Oh, you still want to talk about your waking dreams, huh? All right. Sometimes talking about them is good. Society? It is not a zombi word within our language. We and the outside appear to speak the same language but here we have clear definitions for our words. Outside, definitions are no more than an attempt to record popular usage; that makes sleep-talking acceptable. By sleep-talking I mean using words without having clear, conscious thoughts behind the words. Word connotations preclude clear thought in the outside world.

"Society, the same word, obviously means something different to me and the people here than it does to you. You use the term 'competitive societies.' People here would never say that. Also, unless they were as familiar as I am with outside language, they would not recognize the zombi confusion behind what you were trying to say. To the people here, society means the aggregate of individuals to which each individual relates — and nothing more. 'Competitive societies' implies groups of individuals, who think of themselves as a group entity, striving against other individuals, who think of themselves as a group entity.

"You are still sleep-talking in the language of the world you left. In your waking consciousness you have already accepted the thought patterns on which our agreements are built. Our agreements are between individuals. In the thought pattern here, no human semi-organisms made up of an aggregate of humans, exists as a present reality. We think it would be highly undesirable to create such a group entity. So we have no words, and no word connotations, that would tend toward the concept of such a thing as a desirable creation.

"We know that outside there is a tendency, which is older than human history, toward making an aggregate of discrete individuals into a group organism. It can be done. Ants, termites, and some species of bees have done it. The widespread push toward that tendency is the reason why we cannot relate to the outside world. We *consciously* reject every thought pattern that adds to, or merely perpetuates, such a tendency.

"You know that groups striving against other groups could not happen within the thought patterns underlying our agreements. Competitive societies implies groups of people wherein the group has a will of its own. We recognize that zombis look upon a group as having a will that individuals within the group should accept as having the prerogative to overrule their own."

After I have thought about our conversation these last two days, what I came up with now seems awfully stupid, but I want to put it down so that I can remember my attitude. I said, "Your society — *our* society here — is very different from the outside world. Both want to be the finest possible. Is that not competition?"

I feel sure he likes me and doesn't want to hurt me unnecessarily. I could see him ponder a moment for a way to be kind without being dishonest. He seemed to look over the rubble-strewn wasteland of my mind for a way to contact me, then finally said, "Humans coin words to perpetuate their abstract thoughts. Outside, abstractions are insinuated into language without anyone recognizing that a thought can create a word, and a word is a further step toward creating a reality. A word that assumes the existence of a non-existent group entity is a step toward creating a group entity.

"Here we know ourselves to be conscious creators. We feel responsible for distinguishing between perception and conception. We feel the need to become thoroughly acquainted with existent realities before we create new ones. Here we don't think the mere fact that an idea can be followed intellectually is sufficient justification for inserting a word perpetuating the abstraction into common language. We recognize that language can become a highly effective step toward making a future reality for the human species. We think it highly important that the reality that could be created from the abstract be seen within the total framework of creating a *desirable* future reality before the abstraction is introduced into the language.

"Our language here and the language in the outside world appear to be the same but our thought patterns here and those

80

outside are not the same at all. The world we share with what you have known outside is tangible reality. As tangible realities, as flesh and blood humans, we do not compete with the outside world. We segregate ourselves completely; we don't relate."

"If you — if *we* here — did relate would there be competition?"

"No. If those outside sought to force the relationship on us, we would try to escape from it, try to maintain our separation. If we could not do so, those in the outside world would destroy us."

"You mean kill us? I find that hard to believe."

"Kill us, put us in jail, interbreed with us, require us to send our children to their schools, or, simply, by the pressure of constant, widespread sleep-talking destroy our ability to hold a direction opposed to the one they are going."

"Is that direction," I asked, "so different that you call it destroying us. Are we not all human beings? Are we here some sort of mutation? Are they outside a different species?"

"As a culture, we are a small group different from the big world. But I don't think that we here should be viewed as the mutation; the direction of the outside world is the direction that would make for mutation. If they continue in the direction they are going, if they arrive at the place for which they are now heading, *they* will become a *radically* different species from us. By us I mean present day humans who approve, who say "yes" to what we now are.

"The only direction of life that our reason can say we should choose is the long range direction that we can see as being pointed by the billions of years that life has been evolving. The outside world is not moving further in the direction life has been going for three billion years. It is moving backward. During all the time for which there is any written history, the dominant portion of the outside world has been deviating from total organic life's long range direction — from the direction that *produced* the human species. The outside world is moving in a clearly defined backward direction that would reach no point of stabilization until it had backed up to the point life passed about 600 million years ago, or whenever it was that sex became the newly introduced theme of life's movement in the universe of time.

"The condition on which the outside world would reach stabilization is clear. It would destroy sex. The condition is clear because there is a clear precedent. Ants, termites, and some species of bees have gone all the way in that reverse direction; they have passed the point of no return. They have gone from individuals that func-

81

tion as two sexes to group entities that are asexual. When the group became the functioning entity, the individuals then functioned exclusively as asexual cells in the asexual group. The evidence supplied by ants, termites, and bees clearly shows that the regressive direction results in biological mutation; it makes a new species wherein the individuals can no longer function alone.

"Our direction here calls for no mutation. Everything, without exception, about the human species as it is — when freed from the outside world's brainwashing — fits our present way of life, and it fits our direction for future development. We want to develop ourselves biologically and temperamentally in the pattern already established."

I told him I was so lost that I didn't even know how to ask the right questions, but that I didn't see the difference between us and the outside world clearly by comparing the outside people to the social insects.

After a moment's thought, he asked me, "When you remember the outside world, now, after you have been here as long as you have, what do you find most undesirable about it?"

Almost immediately, I answered, "Mass warfare."

It was the first time I had ever said anything that seemed to surprise him. He looked at me as if he might have missed something about me that could explain such an answer. It obviously did not fit the train of his thoughts. I don't know what his own thoughts were; but he paused, reoriented himself, and said, "All right. Let's start from there. Mass warfare is a unique thing, practiced by humans in the outside world and by what you call the social insects — but by no other animals. Is that the way you see it?"

"I had never thought of it that way," I told him. "How about wolves that attack in packs. And herd animals — caribou and buffalo — where the fighting males form an outside protection for the shielded females and young?"

"The wolf packs are seeking food by cooperative action, and the herd animals are cooperatively protecting themselves against being eaten," he commented. "Together they are doing what each individual would do alone. Is that the way you see mass warfare?"

"No," I told him. "Humans are more complicated and concerned with things beyond food. Wars are fought over differences in religion, politics, abstract theories of economics, and all such things that wolves and buffaloes don't think about."

"How about what you call the social insects?" he asked, and

added that they are called "regressive" insects here. "Do they think more like outside humans than wolves and caribou do? Have they become competitive societies?"

He didn't push for an answer; he waited and gave me time to think. After I had thought it through, I said, "I can see that they depend on the group entity exclusively; they live and die as part of it. Even though they are separate individuals when looked at as physical objects with empty space between them, they no longer function except as part of the group entity."

He nodded agreement, and said, "The wolf pack and the buffalo herd take a tentative step in that direction, but they retain their innate sexuality as individuals. They do not become asexual "cells" or "citizens" of a group entity. The regressive insects have already gone all the way. The outside humans are moving in that direction so rapidly *and with such force* that it appears to be hopeless for the few of us here to try to stop them. Commitment to manipulated groups as the units of power has pushed zombis beyond the stage of reason. But here we have all decided that we don't want to go their way. We don't see it as continuing life's overall direction; we see it as turning back in the direction we have already come."

"Do you think the ants and bees consciously chose their *regressive* direction?" I asked him.

"No," he told me. "And I don't think the people in the outside world are consciously choosing theirs. Both show the same pattern of confusion. The ants and bees got confused by sex odors. Words serve the same purpose of confusing humans in the outside world. Words overrule thought in the field of abstracts that you mentioned — religion, politics, theories of economics, et cetera. Words overrule thought with unexamined connotations that do the same as sex odors in the regressive insects. Connotation of words, rather than conscious thought expressed by words, causes individuals to identify themselves with a group that is already functioning as a semi-organism."

After considering a moment, I *thought* I understood. I could see what he was saying about *others*. I was not looking at myself as a zombi. I even felt complimented because he had leaped over what would have been intermediate explanatory steps.

"Yes," I told him. "I think I understand what you are saying about word connotations that are little more than attractive odors. I was fortunate in being brought up by agnostic grandparents. I had Catholic, Jewish, and Protestant friends but they gave up telling me about all the comfort and satisfaction they found in their religions. Remembering them, I can see that words solemnly intoned in impressive ceremonies can be built up into something that brings people together, and holds them together — as sex odors could. Also I'm fully aware that some of the bloodiest wars have been fought by groups fighting over the odor of words — not over any sense in what the words were saying. Whether because of my grandparents, or because I was lucky to be born with some innate intelligence, I'm not sure, but I never accepted the existence of Jahweh, Jehovah, Allah, or any of the other words with a supernatural — or maybe a supersexual — odor."

He raised his eyebrows skeptically and smiled gently at me. "Even when you were still outside," he said, "you could see some of your friends as zombis who had given over direction of themselves to a hypothesized will outside themselves — a hypothesized will expressed in words cleverly designed to hide the real will doing the group manipulating. Then you were, and now you still are, proud that you accepted no direction from words purported to come from stone idols or invisible gods. But did you not — without recognizing that it was exactly the same thing — accept direction from a nation, or a state, or a 'duly constituted government bureau?' "

I felt as if I had been hit and knocked sprawling. I was no longer a spectator looking back at the outside world, while talking as an equal with a wise old man — while even laughing with him at the self I was now leaving behind. I saw myself as being still a zombi.

And I gave further evidence that I still was. I protested the difference between gods and governments.

But he would not accept it. He said, "A world of people submitting to the control of imaginary things or imaginary beings is what I see — in my waking consciousness — as a world of zombis. It makes little difference to me what kind of imaginary things to which they submit, nor the extent to which they profess belief in their reality. The effect as it concerns one who wants to escape from overpowering groups of individuals who are obeying a purported will, not their own, is all the same. They are not humans that can be met and reasoned with as individuals. They are word controlled zombis."

As he probed my childhood training, I was surprised to remember that I had accepted, with never a thought of questioning it, that the settlers of the *Mayflower,* who had been brainwashed by a thousand years under a theocracy, did not feel that they could set foot on a new soil and begin a new life until they had assembled on shipboard and "formed themselves into a body politic for the direction of their affairs."

He asked me if I believed in the existence of a "body politic." I found that I had accepted it as "something everyone understood" and had never thought about it. He asked me to define it. I made several stabs and realized that I failed, not because I lacked the words but because my concept was not clear. He came to my aid by suggesting that I review the legal definition of a corporation, which he said my "schoolgirl catechism" may have included. I had only a vague idea but I tried to phrase it in legal terms. I said something like, "A corporation is a fictitious entity that can own property, buy, sell, sue, and be sued in the courts, and stand before the law in all respects as if it were a natural person."

"A fictitious entity that can 'stand before the law,' " he repeated. "Even the legal definition has the fictitious entity actually standing up in the court room as if it were a natural person. And what is the 'law' before which it stands? The 'law' is the record of words spoken by another fictitious entity. The judge is proclaiming the existence of the fictitious entity and speaking for it, just as the priests of your friends spoke for their gods."

As he talked I got the picture of zombis, all claiming to be speaking for fictitious entities, meeting in court rooms, and at international conference tables. I could imagine the shadowy non-existent "bodies politic" hovering over the real persons — if we can still call zombis "real persons." The phantoms were everything; the zombis were nothing. And I knew that the fate of millions upon millions of flesh and blood humans could be decided by words the zombis wrote down who were playing out the make-believe conference of phantoms.

Hans, watching me get the real picture of the outside world said, "The people would say that they are not so primitive as to think the fictitious entities actually exist, but they constantly live, talk, think, and act as if they did. Every day there are cartoons of them in the newspapers. There is the familiar cartoon figure of a bear with a hammer and sickle drawn on it and a giant called Uncle Sam. There are cartoons of a giant, representing a big nation, holding a smaller one on his knee as a ventriloquist's dummy, while the more powerful one talks through the mouth of the other. The variations are endless, and all the people outside understand and accept it. Their lives are totally controlled by these phantoms

— phantoms that they think themselves too sophisticated to believe actually exist."

He paused to let me remember what I had known. He gave me time to see it as he saw it.

"Their belief or non-belief in the reality of fictitious entities may be of interest to psychiatrists," he continued, "but their belief or non-belief makes little difference to one whose being or lifestyle is being destroyed by zombis acting on orders coming from some fictitious entity. And it makes little difference whether they think the orders come from a stone idol, an invisible god, or a 'duly constituted civil authority.' The specific form of zombi conditioning ceases to matter when one is confronted by the force of those whose actions need no other reason than the catechism, 'I was just carrying out my orders.' Humans with such conditioning are zombis beyond the reach of human reason."

Over and over he had implied that the parallel between the distorted use of sex odors by the regressive insects and the distorted use of words by humans was much closer than it appeared on the surface. He often implied, or actually stated, that a distorted view of sex was the major factor in creating a fictitious entity, and that sex, itself, was the major obstacle to actual development of a group entity. He said that those trying to create group entities, the mass-manipulators behind the development of churches and states, took great pride in making clever use of sex — the one formidable obstacle that stood in their way. He said that they worked at devising ways to turn the love between men and women into love of some god, church, or state. They had ceremonies in which the nuns gave themselves in marriage to a confused "spiritual" concept of a Christ or church. He said that the males were pushed toward a homosexual thought pattern by encouraging an identity-subordination to a hypothesized god, or some spiritual or political leader of the same sex. The idea was always to separate the *love* based on sex from the physical sexual act. "Love," reduced to an abstract with a vagueness that made it manipulative, became a word having a sex odor that could be used by word speaking humans in exactly the same way the sex odor, itself, had been used by the regressive insects.

"And then," he said, "When there is no concept left of what was the glory of sex except the bare act of sexual intercourse, the church or state embroideries the role of pimp, that it has taken on, with elaborate ceremonies and calls being a pimp: 'Giving a woman to a man in marriage.' "

I asked him, "Just how would you define marriage in words that zombis understand?"

He looked at me sharply for a moment. I suppose it was because I had so much trouble composing that question that the thought passed through his mind that I might be baiting him. Of course I wasn't and I think he quickly dismissed the thought and paused to compose the answer he gave me.

He laughed. "You want to test my ability to speak zombi language. O.K. Marriage is a negotiated sexual relationship wherein the partners tacitly admit that some phantom called church or state has real existence as a volitionary entity, and the phantom has the prerogative to inject itself into the relationship between the man and the woman, and into the relationship between them and their children."

That seemed to clarify the attitude here a lot for me. My ability to fully appreciate his definition gave me a renewed confidence in my school-girl intellect, and I asked him to define sex.

He sighed and was silent a long time before he answered: "Our attitude toward sex is a *major* difference between here and the world outside. Here we think we know the meaning of sex; the world outside is filled, like a kaleidoscope, with the appearance of sex in distorted perspectives and refuses to consider its meaning. Those in the outside world will not accept the meaning that seems obvious to us. They will not accept it because such acceptance would *condemn* group dominance over the individual. The outside world offers no meaning for sex. In all the thousands of years that mass manipulators have been searching for some pseudo-meaning of sex that will support their movement toward forming group entities, they have not been able to come up with anything that might appear plausible. Everyone in the outside world now merely says that sex is an accident of nature that continued to develop because it made for faster evolution of sexual organisms and therefore dominance of sexual animals over the asexual.

"I can define marriage in words because it is something created by men. It was created by primitive men whose limits of intelligence and perception I can encompass and evaluate. Sex is something entirely different. Sex is a reality — a development running through all nature throughout the whole world for millions upon millions of years before the human species came into existence. I could use words for hours to point out what I perceive as significant facets of it, but a word *definition* of sex, or of any natural reality, would be more than I would presume to make. Words can only be used to point to limited views of reality.

"I could use words to talk about attitudes toward sex. But if I used words to point to the facets of sex that I imagine you have known in the outside world, I'm afraid it might be too much for you, a brand plucked from the burning, to accept about a whole people of whom you can have no other than good memories. You are still bound to them by pleasant emotional attachments. I think you would do well to move into our life here slowly enough so that your intellect and your emotions can both move in at the same pace.

"For now I suggest that you examine the radical difference between our yes-saying to sex here and the pressure of the outside world to destroy it, as that difference can be seen by comparing our agreements between individuals to the laws purportedly coming from hypothesized group entities that govern the lives of zombis outside."

I guess he is right. I get a glimpse of something that I suspect is there. But I don't yet really see any big significant statement about sex being made by looking at the simple individual agreements here. I, of course, do recognize that, in actual practice, the simple agreements here are far better than the garbage pile of laws that faces people in the outside world.

I'm glad that I have time to think about all this, to think about what is happening to me, and to write down my thoughts and experiences. This writing things down helps me a lot.

15.

Yesterday was warm and the world smelled good. Kirk was falling and cutting up some trees for firewood, and as I don't have the strength or skill to use an ax — and thought he wanted to be alone anyway — I took a long walk.

Finding a road alongside a creek I followed it until I came to what looked like a miniature of an old mill. There was a fully operating waterwheel being turned by the stream. When I got there I found Bingee, Inger, and Lolena relaxing in the sun with the water from the falls running over their feet. They had been watching me and my puzzlement about what I had found. As soon as I saw them, they invited me to pull off my shoes and join them. In a lazy, casual way they seemed glad to see me, so I accepted their invitation. The water was cold and felt good.

The mill, one that Dag had helped make when he was young, is now used and maintained by our group, and the girls had come down to see if anything needed repair after the winter. But everything was in good order so they just turned their trip into full enjoyment of lazy relaxation on a beautiful day.

I spent the whole afternoon with them. It was a wonderful time, a mood of relaxing and coming into rhythm with the running water, white clouds moving across a blue sky, growing trees and the slowly turning mill wheel. I don't need to write about that, or about the good feel I got about the whole place here from that lazy afternoon with the girls; I know it will always come back as a sort of remembered melody that I would never even try to put into words. But I picked up a lot of information about this place that I do want to write down.

Each piece of the jigsaw puzzle that goes into place relieves a little more my early fears that I was lost and alone. Now the world around me seems to be filling in solidly, and the more I see the better I like it. Also I like the feeling of solidity itself, the feeling that this place has extension in space and has a history that will somewhere join that of the world I knew, and will then put a solid past behind me.

Camp 38 is a much bigger place than I thought from my first day of talking with the children and from what I have seen. It includes a lake sixteen kilometers across where a group of people live who seem to have a lot of fun with canoes and sailboats. Inger, Bingee and Lolena sometimes visit, enjoy the lake and the boats; and the people from the lake sometimes come here. Riding is a novel experience for the people from the lake. No one there raises horses or cattle. Fish is a big part of their diet and their clothes are mostly of flax, which they grow and turn into cloth by using waterpower from a creek for spinning wheels and looms. The lake is thirty kilometers from here.

Camp 38 also extends to the ocean which is over seventy kilometers away.

Everyone here seems to know the physical geography of the world thoroughly, but to know nothing of political geography or history as I know it — the history of nations. Institutional education on the outside sounds like prison and brainwashing when I hear about it from children, but Inger, Bingee, and Lolena seem to have a very accurate knowledge of what life is like outside. They don't relate to nations, but they have the usual names for continents thought of as physical geography. They pay no attention to politics; they don't even distinguish between life in America, Europe, and Asia. However they do recognize that there are differences between the conditions of life among poor struggling people; among those who play for power in the mixed-deck game of money, politics, and religion; and among the masses of comfortable, unthinking status seekers who keep the mechanics of the world going. Although entirely capable of conceiving extreme poverty and immense wealth, they appear unimpressed by either.

Their ideas of the people outside are quite realistic. Although the word zombi seems to have the same connotations for them that it has for me, they have less unreasoned emotional bias against zombis than most Americans have against citizens of other countries. They have no idea that I am much less a zombi than others and they like and accept me.

There's no general prohibition against anyone leaving here. All think that they will probably go outside sometime. But they are horrified at the idea of falling in love with a zombi. And they think this might happen if they go out while too young. They think that if they went outside they would certainly want to come back here and they think a man could not be brought back with as little trouble as Kirk brought me. There are a few exceptions, of which Kirk's father was one, but few men are brought in and the conviction that bringing men in won't usually work is very widespread. The girls think about it and agree. They asked me to think of the men I knew outside and consider whether they could be brought in as I was. I thought about it and I feel sure that not a single one would work out. But at the same time I think most of the men and boys I have known and liked would have chosen this in preference to the outside world as a life to be born to. I should think about that paradox sometime. There are so many things to think about I will never get caught up. Solitude — time to think has become a very real necessity. And the fact that I can have it is like having great wealth.

How people are kept out of here is the real puzzle to me. I thought we were a fairly small spot hidden in the woods and, since we didn't disturb anyone, maybe no one paid any attention to us. But when I found out the size of Camp 38 the idea of simply hiding out seemed fantastic. I asked the girls about it but they weren't much help. They admitted that we're not simply inconspicuous. They even volunteered the information that the planes which can sometimes be seen flying over are capable of taking pictures that show all details. But, admitting all this, they still seemed to think the puzzle not much of a puzzle. However the only explanation offered me was that the zombis who know about us don't interfere and the zombis who would interfere don't know.

It was a good afternoon — an enormously good afternoon. For a long time we lay around talking about the things at the edge of knowledge that are so important but usually get little conscious attention. We talked leisurely and intimately about our relationship to the sky, the sun, the clouds, the water, the earth, the trees; it was the most relaxing and personality in depth revealing contact I have had with this trio. Apparently the girls are such natural pagans that they can have no distorted concepts of reality. They move from art and emotion to reason — from what Hans called dreams to waking consciousness — with no danger of losing their way.

Giving themselves fully to dreams while retaining consciousness, they talked about how peaceful and content the sky must "feel" today. They talked about how the wind "feels," how it feels to be blue like the sky, green like the trees, or at rest like the rocks. They came fully back into conscious reality as I know it when they focused on a nearby tree. It was on the creek bank where it was exposed to the wind and had also been half undermined by the creek during a winter flood. It was looked upon as another person. It was admired as a personality who had withstood the wind in its branches and the water washing its roots; and it was remembered as an old friend. Shallow sentimentality was utterly unknown to them. They were simple and factual but they looked at the tree as a living thing like themselves. They just talked of how the branches on one side, compensating for the wash of the soil, had grown very vigorously the last three years and now, having accomplished the shift of weight, the tree was putting out new branches on the other side this year. They didn't have an I-it relationship with the tree; it was I-thou. However there was no existentialism which has to send long delicate roots through a civilization's sophistry to reach reality; they were utterly free of sophistry; they were pagan.

I recognized that this paganism was not a primitive religion; it was an intellectual advance beyond the present perspective of Western science. The girls' knowledge of weather, geology, botany, and the intricate interrelation between plants, birds, insects, soil, water, and air was so far ahead of mine that I could only enter into the conversation as a child listening to adults tries to think of some worthwhile contribution, or not too silly question to ask, so he can hug to himself the feeling of belonging. They knew every tree and plant and bird by name. With some I was well enough acquainted

91

to know the names they used were those used in Western science. When I tested with my scant knowledge, I felt sure they knew plant and animal families, species, and genera by the names they would be called in the general scientific world.

After feeling the two worlds draw closer I got a jar at discovering a new difference. I was lying on my back with my arms under my head, feeling how completely I belonged, and I said, "I've lost all track of time since I've been here." Then suddenly, in the middle of what would have been an idle check up of dates, I found that the calendar here is utterly different from the one I know. Months have the familiar names but they are shorter than months I know, refer entirely to moon phases, and are not used to count time. Time is counted by seasons only. This is the thirty-fourth day of spring. And this is the year one hundred and forty-one. Time dates from the first people here.

The girls can talk circles around me on astronomy but they make a symbolism of the mathematical incompatibility between the phases of the moon and the earth's orbit around the sun that sounds utterly primitive. However I recognize that it is not super-stition but art motifs transformed into a symbolism for advanced communication. The moon takes on a feminine character and the sun a masculine character. There is a festive season, Selentag, made of the twelve days around the first full moon after the winter solstice that has about it the suggestion of formally honoring the feminine temperament. A man would be very reluctant to challenge another man during this time because attention is given to the "light in the darkness" which refers both to the moon and to woman. I couldn't find out whether this is a conscious revival of a pre-Christian concept of Christmas or not because the girls don't relate to Christianity. Gifts are not generally given during this period but, because there is a lot of interrelation between everyone at this time, incidental gift giving takes place. On the whole, having useless possessions is looked upon as sloppiness; gifts are never given unless the giver's knowledge that the recipient wants them is beyond question. The festive season is a time of open house by everyone. It is really two related periods, divided by a noon to noon total pause in moving about for visiting on the night of the full moon. Visitors at one place remain as house guests during this interval. During the first period the adults and small children hold open house and adolescents visit. During the next period adoles-cents hold open house and adults and small children visit. I can see planning and purpose behind the festival but the symbolism of woman and moon surprises me a little. Apparently I'm going to have to expand my concept of art because I know that this sort of thing can't be superstition here.

Now that I think of art, I remember that I have some orientation in art concepts coming up this summer. I don't quite know what to make of it yet. The girls are going to be "wildsmaidens" in an "opera" about the fifteenth day of summer. The exact date could vary because it will be outdoors and four night of good weather are needed. They didn't want to tell me much because they wanted it all to be new to me. I found out about it by accident.

I was trying to find out more about why they don't want to have anything to do with the outside world if everyone here is free to come and go, and Inger said that if people and zombis got all mixed up again it would be very difficult to keep the children from becoming zombis. "Some of the adults might even be affected," she said and then repeated what apparently is a chief concern: "I —any of us — might fall in love with a zombi."

"It would be like 'The Downfall of the Gods,' " Bingee injected, "when the gods and dwarfs got all mixed up and Siegfried was killed and all the gods were destroyed."

"Valerie hasn't been here long enough to see the opera," Lolena reminded. Then she turned to me and said, "You'll like that. It's about the fifteenth day of summer. Inger, Bingee and I will be the wildsmaidens this year."

"Do you mean the opera written by Wagner?" I asked. "And do you mean Rhinemaidens instead of wildsmaidens?"

"No, I mean wildsmaidens," she insisted. "Maidens from the wilds. The opera was written by Kirk's father."

"I think that isn't quite right, Lolena," Inger told her. "Kirk's father rewrote the words, but the original words and the music as we know it was written by an outsider named Wagner. He was half awake and, as he played with the old myths, he let his subconscious speak against zombiism. Of course the zombis didn't understand. They even like the opera as it is given in zombiland. If I guess right, that's why you know it, isn't it, Valerie?"

I told them that the opera was frequently given outside but confessed that I knew very little about it and had never seen it. They said that they should tell me nothing so it would all be a surprise. I think I got across my enthusiasm and interest in knowing more and at the same time showed my willingness to let them change the subject. In the course of the day we talked about almost everything.

There obviously was a lumber camp here eighty or ninety years ago and the name Camp 38 comes from that. The girls didn't simply say that there had been a logging operation and assume the understanding people would assume outside. At that time, in the language of the girls, "a lot of zombis moved in and lived in flimsy little houses all crowded up against each other. They brought in all their food and clothes from the outside and no one did anything but cut down trees and send them out to zombiland. Most of the zombis left but a few of them stayed and became people."

What interests and puzzles me is that everything from the outside is *fully absorbed* and becomes part of the way of life here or it is *totally rejected*. I can't imagine what brings that about. Putting together what I learned from them and what I learned about educational methods here the other day, I am beginning to get a feeling that there has been a definite purpose and direction in the development of this place, but the history is still very hazy to me.

I told Kirk about the significant points of my conversation with the girls last night and he confirmed everything they told me, including their opinion that I would enjoy it more if I don't learn about the opera until time to see it. I asked if we could visit the people at the lake and also if we could go to the ocean sometime. He readily agreed. We will probably do both before the summer is over.

16.

Today my zombi intellect wants to take over my writing. I think my emotions are now tied tight enough to the reality here for me to let my zombi intellect have its fling. I want to think about professor Kane and my old classmates majoring in anthropology and the impulse doesn't disturb me. But relations have changed. In these few short weeks I have run on ahead of my classmates. I have even bypassed some of my professors. Today I'm anxious to do my doctorate thesis. Proposition: A major function of law courts is something aside from administration of laws; it is satisfaction of a social requirement.

Yesterday I spent all day at the seasonal Forum, and, after my new idea about a court of law impressed me, everything before me seemed to stand out as evidence in support of my proposition.

Outwardly the Forum looks to me and my zombi conditioning like a law court. Looking with the eyes of an outsider, I could see a judge, a claimant and a defendant, their attorneys, a clerk of the court, and all the trappings and solemnity of a court trial. Although the counterparts have different names here, cases are called before the "judge" by a "clerk;" there are witnesses, cross examinations, objections from alert attorneys which are overruled or sustained; both sides of the case are pleaded; and a "judgment" is handed down from the bench.

Maybe instead of writing my doctorate thesis I should be doing a magazine article so I could slip up on the difference between the Forum and a court for dramatic effect.

First. Although "criminal" cases come before the Forum, always, as in "civil" cases outside, the "prosecuting attorney" is the attorney for the claimant. There is no one acting for the "state," the "people," or the "crown."

Second. When the "judge" has "passed judgment" he calls for dissenting opinions and yields the bench for dissenting "judgments."

Third. The "judgment" has absolutely no force whatsoever as law does outside. While the Forum is in session a temporary sign hangs alongside the permanent brass plaque reciting the seven points of agreements between individuals, which is on the wall behind the "judge." The temporary sign reads: "This is a discussion Forum. It is not a trial where individuals have agreed to accept the judgment of others as overruling their own. Agreements to submit differences to this Forum and to accept the advice *before* that advice has been given have been construed as violation of the fifth agreement between individuals." Reference to a specific case is added.

Since any violation of the formal agreements carries the death penalty, it took only one such case to stop any tendency to let the Forum evolve into an institution for making laws.

With the similarities and differences set forth, the significant thing is that the Forum does not degenerate into a ludicrous parody of a law court. It does not. It has a valid function that entitles it to intellectual appreciation. The function is not that of enforcing "laws." The term "agreements" here is not simply another word substituted for "laws." I thought so at first but now I see the radical difference in the basic concept. The notice alongside the agreements emphasizes the difference. The function of the Forum is that of providing a formal conversation between society and the individual.

The feeling of dignified and weighty consideration that the traditional court atmosphere provides is an ideal form through which the function can find expression. The individual who is uncertain of his position with regard to a society, composed of many people whom he may not know as individuals, often needs to have himself formally recognized, to have his problems acknowledged, and to hear a solemn, considered opinion regarding them expressed by society — because this society, as a totality, does often have a continuing existence as an entity, *at least in his dreams.* Here the Forum is allowed to articulate the dream entity in a form that makes it easy for waking consciousness to recognize, study it, and make a conscious decision about how the concerned individual relates to the whole. Here society meets the individual under conditions where he is not simply a pawn that can be pushed around for the purpose of giving those who identify with society an ego-flattering feeling of oneness — a oneness that is bigger, more powerful, and wiser than the individual who has the problem. Here the participating persons who constitute society must have individual courage rather than mob courage. Further, it is upon the individuals acting as individuals that the court depends for its dignity.

A court that had no respect-demanding force behind it would immediately degenerate into a farce. Outside it is the court that has the power, and it is the court which enforces the dignity. Here the individual has all the force of society behind him because everyone has agreed to support individual sovereignty. So it is the individual who enforces the dignity of the Forum.

There is one case on record of a "judge" who, when a seeming trivial problem was brought before him, could not resist making some humorously ridiculing remark at which the whole assembly burst into laughter. The claimant had been living alone so long that he had apparently lost his sense of humor. He issued a challenge to the "judge" and killed him in formal combat.

For those who need a reminder, one case like that brings home the knowledge that each individual's problems are of vital importance to him.

I didn't give much attention to the actual cases yesterday, partly because I was absorbed in my thoughts about the whole, and partly because none of them seemed very serious. Most of them seemed to be ones brought up by people who had tended to isolate themselves. There was one in which a challenge had already been issued and bringing the problem before the Forum averted combat. It was two men in a remote area squabbling over pollution of a stream when a solution fully acceptable to both was common knowledge. The weight of public opinion as to what was an equitable way of meeting the situation was all that was necessary. Two attorneys *who were interested in arriving at a solution rather than winning their cases,* questioned and cross questioned the opponents in a way that displayed and fully articulated the insignificant misunderstandings on which they had built their hostility. The opposing parties reached a solution and asked to have the case dismissed before the presiding advisor (the title used instead of judge) had handed down an opinion.

There was one other charge that may have been serious. It was a charge for mistreatment brought by a twelve year old boy against his father. The father did not appear before the Forum and defend himself. The boy could show no physical evidence of mistreatment but the advisor, anticipating a possible action by the father against the boy, asked for a volunteer to visit him, let him know that interest had been aroused, and advise him that if the boy had no commerce with friends and neighbors, restraint, that constituted breaking the first point of the agreements, would be suspected and investigated.

Often the season Forum lasts several days and because of the seriousness of the cases the assembly house is sometimes packed to overflowing. Special sessions are often called. Yesterday was a regular quarterly Forum but all cases were completed in one day, and most of them were squabbles by people who simply needed the sounding board of public opinion to help them decide on acceptable conduct. Two or three cases even came in the class that I would have called "advice to the lovelorn."

I will undoubtedly become interested in individual cases as I become better acquainted, but yesterday I was almost totally interested in the fact that such an institution could exist. So far as I know, it is the only one of its kind that ever has existed. I was fully absorbed in what its existence means.

The mechanics of the whole thing seem highly significant to me. The women who choose to rotate as clerks in the assembly house apparently do a lot more than I originally thought. They keep the files of what appears before the Forums as well as the trials of those accused of breaking their agreements. They also have files of those who have said they would be available as advisors or attorneys and the kind of cases in which they are interested. They give notice of and arrange for special Forums. They have quite a bit of influence in giving preliminary advice and bringing together parties of the cases and appropriate attorneys. They fill out the cards when the cases are scheduled before the Forum and later complete them to show their disposition. Then they keep them as permanent records.

Such women have their counterparts in every society, but usually their influence goes on behind the scenes. Here, as elsewhere, they keep their fingers on the pulse of the community activities and contribute their benign smiles or discouraging frowns. Here they do it openly and formally.

Advisors and attorneys are all volunteers. No qualifications are necessary except a willingness to serve and acceptance by the parties involved. Advisors and attorneys don't even have to be sovereign. Of course attorneys don't have to be acceptable to the opposing side but a presiding advisor has to be acceptable to both whenever both sides are heard.

Several available advisors sit in a box like a jury and sometimes give dissenting opinions. They ask the presiding advisor for permission to speak. The presiding advisor conveys the request and receives the approval of both parties before allowing an advisor in the box to speak. Great honor is attached to being repeatedly selected by both sides as presiding advisor.

An attorney also has honor and the fact that this is adequate motivation was brought home to me intimately. I was surprised and wide-eyed with admiration and envy to see Inger come forward and present a case as an attorney. My impression of her assured bearing and competence, I believe, will stay with me as long as I live. I think it highly significant that a big part of that impression was my awareness that a "career" as an attorney, for which her handling of the case showed her extremely well-fitted, would appear to her as an unthinkable degradation. To her this was just another part of being a well-rounded person.

The conversation between society and the individual is not only between society and the claimant or defendant but between society and everyone who participates. And, in a one way conversation, society also speaks to the passive spectator.

I decided yesterday while I was sitting in the Forum that, since the items of agreement here are so few and simple, and since the death penalty for violations eliminates habitual "criminals," this institution had to come into being for a purpose which is not that of enforcing laws designed to maintain social order. Historically a court room is a circus of the Caesars. In the outside world the court room trial has already taken over from the parades of captives taken in war and the barbaric contests in the coliseum. Here the contests that push one into a desire for identity with society are gone, and a facet of the court room trial re-appears on a higher plateau. No dream-identity of the individual with the all-powerful oneness of mob force is pampered and formally approved. This is a field of decisions made by waking consciousness. Here what appears to be a law court has become an institution for social communication in this higher civilization.

I think I could fully support my limited proposition in a doctorate thesis but I'm not yet ready to make a conclusion about the ultimate meaning of what I saw in the Forum as an institution. According to the ideas that I accepted without real examination when I was at school, primitive man identifies himself almost totally with society. As he becomes more conscious, he begins to separate himself from the group and become an individual.

If this viewpoint is accepted, the question arises as to whether, as an individual, he then begins a conversation with society, which becomes increasingly necessary as the difference between him and society is widened. Or does he ultimately free himself completely from the concept of society as a totality and have converse only with other individuals?

And, is the Forum here a transitional institution that will gradually fade until it disappears completely, or is the need it satisfies a continuing one which must always find satisfaction in one form or another?

17.

The memory that I have ever known any life other than this has ceased to be more than an intellectual puzzle for me. I would just as soon forget the other world. I feel as I am sure one does who goes to a long dreamed of resort for a two week's vacation; he would just as soon forget the customary seven-thirty alarm clock, the eight-thirteen commute train, and the dash from the train so as to get to the office by nine o'clock. I sometimes think of my old dependence on radio and TV but I don't long for any part of the things I remember. Sometimes I think of Peggie and wonder if she is all right, but I know there would be little I could do for her if I were still living with her. So I put away that one emotionally close memory and, except as a puzzle of the relation between the two worlds, the rest goes away of itself.

This is my reality and it gives me a life emotionally fuller of the things I want then I ever dreamed it could be. Nothing is gone but the pointless activity of solving meaningless complications in the mechanics of living. The time — the biggest part of sixteen years — that I spent in school appalls me now when I realize that the attention I had to give to ridiculous things is the very reason I am so utterly uneducated. There are few ten year old children here who are not better educated to survive than I. Inger, Lolena, and Bingee are all younger than I, and as to skill in both survival and good living they are far ahead of me. I feel that my position with relation to them is what it would have been if I had wasted at least ten years in some big prison or institution for the feeble minded, doing inconclusive complicated tests so as to provide employment for psychologists and educators. Here I can make no possible use of the junk I spent my time learning.

I like cooking and took two years in school. I can at least cook from basic materials and am not dependent on packaged mixes. In the little smattering I got from a year's course in sewing I can thread a needle and make a few stitches. I know I'm going to have to learn such things as how to make my own patterns for shoes and clothes when I get to the point of needing some. Also I'm going to have to learn to dye and color if I expect to take pride in what I create. But sewing is just a simple part of the things I must learn. Right now I'm struggling with such basic little-child things as how to tell time and direction by the sun or stars and how to tell a vegetable from a weed when it's growing in the ground. Kirk and the girls are extremely helpful but I realize that the biggest lesson I'm learning from them is how to impart information without being dogmatic. Maybe someday I'll have some to impart.

All big jobs here are simply occasions for social contact. Group work isn't necessary. A little of it simply makes life fuller. I like working with Kirk in our vegetables, pruning and caring for fruit trees, caring for the horses and cattle, learning to milk a cow, and learning the temperaments and habits of various animals. We have had another day of working in the fields with the whole group and it was even more fun the second time than the first. Not only have the people taken on a new interest for me because of my further acquaintance with them, I'm also beginning to understand what the work is accomplishing and becoming interested in that.

At another luncheon like the first day of field work I tried to give Margaret an opportunity to acknowledge our zombi bond in some way outside the hearing of others but she simply smiled at me as if she recognized my game and didn't want to play my way. The refusal however was wholly kind. I like her an awful lot and I feel she likes me but she seems to think it wiser to keep away from me.

I see Hans often but, by an unspoken agreement, we never refer to our last conversation or to zombiland. He spends much of his time extracting what he thinks is worthwhile from old zombi books, reorganizing it, and putting it into the language of people. He showed me some of the things he's working on but mostly we talk about tangible realities and things that are happening here and now. I occasionally work with him in his garden and have lunch with him. He's seventy-eight but he loves life with a deep overflowing joy that makes him fun to be around. I'm going to try not to spoil our relationship with any more zombi talk.

After all this time it's hard for me to get back into the mood I had when I started writing about the novelty and strangeness of this place. It no longer seems novel and strange. The other world is beginning to seem strange — almost like a nightmare of mild but interminable and meaningless confusion that I sometimes remember but would just as soon forget. Occasionally something does hit me as surprisingly different from what I retain of the old thought pattern and I suspect that someday, when someone else is brought in, I'll wish I had written down my own reactions. But if I'm going to do so I'm going to have to catch them faster. There's very little that stands out now when I pick up this book again.

My anthropology and its formula of thinking just came back to me. Going over the formula I recall one thing that has impressed me since I last wrote in my diary: the burial of the dead.

One warm afternoon when Kirk and I were walking through the woods, and I'm sure he sensed that I was in an appropriate mood for it, he led me to a particularly beautiful spot where several trees of widely different varieties were growing in a suggestively meaningful relationship to each other. I noticed at once that the natural pattern of the forest had been altered by some unusual cause that wasn't apparent. I was enthusiastic over the beauty of the trees and began to walk around and look at them with growing excitement and wonder at their different ages. I could see that some of the younger trees could have had no parent tree in the vicinity to seed them.

"Someone must have lived here at some time," I conjectured. "These had to be set out deliberately by intelligent beings with a feeling for trees. But there's no sign that there's ever been a house here."

"This is where many people who have meant much to me are buried," he said.

His words brought me up short with a feeling that I might be violating sacred ground. I looked about but saw no tombstones.

He showed me two madrona trees side by side and told me his mother was buried under the larger one and his father under the other. There were two young oak trees with enough space around them for their ultimate growth. Under these were his maternal grandfather and grandmother who had raised him after his parent's death. Both grandparents had died within the last five years. Two mature sturdy oaks identified the graves of his great-grandfather and great-grandmother. Various aunts and uncles were represented by maple, oak, cedar, fir, and various other trees. I remember one holly and one magnolia, both of which marked the graves of women.

The expressed wishes of those dead as to the type of tree they would like to mark their grave had usually been followed and, strangely, so it seemed to me, also their wishes as to the depth of burial. Sometimes bodies are cremated and the ashes buried under a newly planted tree, but the more usual thing is to bury someone in the ground, often, at their expressed wish, without a casket of any kind, and anywhere from two to six feet deep. Some people apparently like the thought of the roots of the tree reaching their bodies before total disintegration. Kirk thought he would probably want for himself a shallow grave and a Douglas Fir tree. In answer to my questioning he said his preferences weren't very strong and his reasons were still too undefined in his own mind to try to explain them. This seemed to be a studied appraisal; he had no reluctance to talk of death and burial. Mostly only very close friends attend the burial. They dig the grave themselves and plant the little trees. There are no formal ceremonies.

"There's nothing to be said to people at large," Kirk explained the lack of ceremony. "Death is each person's most private concern. All those who love someone can do to show respect for the products of his life is what they think he would want done. The decaying body is one of the products as is a house he has built. What others feel or don't feel about it is between each of them alone and the one who's dead." He said that he thought it a bungling crudeness to use the moment of disposing of the body for some ceremony to anesthetize one's feelings or display one's religious beliefs.

"And these trees," I asked, thinking of the sacred groves of the Northern European pagans, "what do you think will eventually happen to them?"

"If someone deliberately mutilated these," he said, "he would have to fight me. What one feels about burial trees won't stand up before waking consciousness, so it would be silly to try to seek agreement about it — to expect respect for one's feeling about it because they were reasonable; we know too little of death. But any man who has feelings about something will demand that others respect his feelings to the extent that they respect him. While I keep these trees in their present condition everyone will recognize that I have some feeling about them so I don't expect to have to fight anyone over disrespect shown them. If at some time the forest is allowed to obliterate this place, presumably there'll be no one alive who cares what happens. Then its purpose will have been served and it won't matter."

He showed me some work he had done on the creek to keep it from changing course and invading the burial grove. I remembered the day he had taken a pick ax and shovel and gone off alone and how I had thought it a little odd that he, who seems incapable of falsity, should, in order to tell me he wanted to be alone with his thoughts, make a pretext of looking after a few favorite trees in the middle of the forest. I was terribly ashamed of my making to myself such an explanation of an action taken by Kirk. Maybe someday I will understand what integrity is and learn to look for honest meanings in what people here say and do.

18.

I realize that I learned various conventions of behavior before I can remember. Later I accepted the explanation that conventions are the oil which keeps society running smoothly. Now I'm beginning to doubt it. Small children here fight as they do anywhere else but they're not fed the oil of conventions. Instead, parents point out to the children the responsibilities they must face as potential sovereigns, and the advantages to be gained by working out good relations with each other. The whole is so simple that it is easily grasped by the child. The child then thinks for himself and develops his own good behavior by voluntarily imitating effective ways of expressing a sincere liking. The absence of enforced contacts with those one doesn't like seems to eliminate bad behavior.

These comments came out because I noticed my last words about Kirk's honesty in little day to day things, and it seemed to tie in, by way of a common childhood training, with the sincere graciousness of the people we visited at the lake. To Kirk they were only casual acquaintances; they had never seen me; but the sincerity of their invitation for Kirk to bring me to visit them, and of our welcome when we arrived was never in doubt. The feeling that there was no superficial behavior which had to be penetrated before one got to the real persons was a surprising and wonderful experience. A connoisseur of fine procelain would feel something of what I felt after being confronted with crude imitations for years and then finding a rare and exquisite original article done by an artist of genuine pride and ability. These people are all original artists in charming behavior.

Everyone at the lake was curious about us, particularly me, in that zombis are so much a rarity that I'm still the newest one here. But their looking at me was frank. It was good to look into their faces because they have learned to love life and the things they see in a completely open manner. There was neither an embarrassed turning away when our eyes met nor any implication that an exchange of smiles asked for or might presume upon further intimacy. Every contact always seemed sufficient in itself.

Wang and Boleen were not expecting us; their invitation had included a positive statement that it was open as to time. If our visit had been inconvenient I'm sure we would have been told so with a studied honesty that is much more wonderful than a child's simplicity.

We arrived in the middle of the afternoon, stayed all night, and until after lunch the next day. Wang, Boleen, and their two children, Gong and Lolinda, four and six years of age were bruising flax and putting it to soak. Wang and Kirk found a place to make the horses comfortable during our stay; the people at the lake have no horses and we had brought our own feed for the horses in the chariot. The children were told we would all have another lunch as soon as they had finished a little pile of work that Boleen laid out to occupy them while she and I went into the house to arrange some juice and rice cakes. She also brought out some cheese and dark bread. After the mid afternoon snack all of us went to work on the flax and worked until almost sundown, finishing all that would be necessary for the next day so we'd have leisure to see everything around the lake together.

Wang is probably half Chinese and half European; he has a

great happiness from his Chinese heritage and a European frame that shows enough muscle and bone to give the whole an effect of quiet joy with enormous depth. Boleen shows the usual mixture of Oriental, American Indian, and European blood but it comes out in a way to make a dark-eyed, round faced hodgepodge that is not pretty but utterly fascinating in the way it's put together; it's impossible to turn away from her and forget that face. She laughs easily and has pretty teeth, although they too are irregular. I wouldn't try to describe the children. If Wang were a composer on the piano he might get them into a little half minute jumble of notes, or I might, if I woke up feeling crazy-happy some morning, try making a festive little holiday dessert with taste surprises in it that would remind me of them. But I couldn't put anything about them down in words.

Although I know it was good I don't remember what we had for dinner. What I remember was the preparation of it. I'm sure that what we ate was fairly simple but cooking it and putting it on the table was like a three ring circus come to town. Kirk, Wang, those two children, and I were all brought into the act from the first moment to the finished crazily decorated table. Boleen, of course, directed; she handed things out with laughter in a song she made up as she went along, until I felt that everything must have gone on the table and come off in a ring half a dozen times, just to keep the circus going. Actually I suspect it was amazingly orderly and efficient — a system she has worked out to amuse the children.

After dinner the children were put to bed and the four of us went sailing on the lake. The lake area was settled because of the good fishing but no one fishes with hooks in the lake any more. They have a community project of raising fish in the stream that enters into the lake over a series of dams they have made. At first the pools behind the dams were used to systematically breed and feed fish and the pool nearest the lake, with the most mature fish, was open to anyone who wanted to dip them up. There are now so many that they are periodically turned into the lake because the younger fish need to be put in the pool before all the older ones are eaten. The lake has so many fish that once or twice a year they spend two or three days seining it. They take the biggest fish and the undesired types and use them to fertilize their already fertile fields.

Everyone knows about the over abundance of fish, and visitors, even strangers, can take as many as they want. There are several places along the lake dedicated to the use of wayfaring strangers where fish may be cooked and there are comfortable shelters from the weather with beautifully designed fireplaces. Kirk and I would have spent the night in one of these if our coming had been at an inconvenient time for Wang and Boleen.

Except for seining the lake when the winds are right and it is a good time to use the fish for fertilizer — early spring and late fall — the canoes and sailboats are used only for enjoying the weather on the lake. Strong, stormy winds entice those who are accustomed to sailing in them onto the lake. The time we were there it was a warm night, a light breeze, and a full moon. There were probably twenty-five small sailing boats out when we were.

It was a wonderful night and place for young love. The frogs and crickets could seldom be heard because there was so much happy laughter coming from the boats. There was a lot of singing, some string instruments and what I thought of as the sounds from shepherds' flutes although the flute notes came from the boats. Somewhere, we never got close to them, there were two silver voiced trumpets calling and answering each other across the lake. I don't know whether they were on shore or in the boats and I have learned that it's crude to ask such things at such a time. The sounds over the lake, and the lights on the water and the surrounding hills from the moon and from several open fires on the shore, were enough to fully occupy our attention.

I've gotten over the ridiculous feeling I once had of a necessity for making conversation, but in my eagerness to know Wang and Boleen I did ask a lot of questions, trying to confine them to subjects that were in keeping with the mood of the evening. Boleen also was full of questions and we sailed and talked until long after midnight. I want to spend another such evening sometime when the newness of everything has worn off enough so that I can enjoy the there and then to the fullest.

The next day we saw the mechanics of life among the people at the lake and talked of the differences between theirs and our ways of living.

After we had seen everything Wang and Kirk seemed to feel it necessary that they discuss — almost argue — about the differences.

We give more time than they think is good to horses and cattle and to the cultivation of large areas required for feeding the big animals.

Kirk said the relation with the big muscled animals and the use of one's own big muscles in slow heavy work was something he had a deep yearning for when he was away from it for any length of time.

Wang valued the greater amount of time to spend on other things — amusing mechanical devices like the water-powered spinning-wheels and looms, irrigation ditches and pumps for the fields. There's a community project of an electric dynamo, tool grinding motors, and vibrating tools that can be used in connection with the flax processing. Also some of the looms have been located away from the creek and powered by electricity. (Except for the electric lights in assembly halls everyone apparently prefers candles to electricity for lighting.) Wang has a feeling that an undreamed of good way of life can be worked out from "playing with zombi toys" (mechanical gadgets). He doesn't feel that his objective is the ridiculous one of simply saving time and work by cleverness when everyone already has all the leisure one wants. He used the joy to be found in a sailboat as a prime example of something good created by a force and will external to it. He said that its function was so completely integrated into its design that it almost had being of itself. He mentioned ice skates and skis, which feature strongly in the winter life of most people here, as other examples of what he was trying to say.

Kirk, agreeing with Wang up to a point, added that all such things might almost be thought of as portals for communion between the organic and inorganic world. I saw a look pass between the two men that made me realize there was a closer understanding between them than appeared on the surface.

The discussion between Wang and Kirk was only a bringing into conscious acceptance the differences in two ways of life. Each was looking for some facet that caused the other to consider his own life better than that of the other. An honest meeting of people getting newly acquainted often takes this direction here. Everyone here apparently agrees on two basic concepts: (1) Man's potential for conscious creative participation in the world of reality puts him in the forefront of evolutionary progress, and (2) specialization to the point of interdependence is dropping back from this forefront position. Within that framework there is no concept of right and wrong living. Differences are loved. They are discussed, even argued about, not to destroy them but to strengthen them, as a tree is strengthened by the wind. If either Wang or Kirk, in arguing a little over their preferences for ways of life, had been convinced that he was wrong both would have felt it was a mutual loss.

When they return our visit Wang, Boleen, and the children will walk. It will probably take them two days to get here. But it would be an insult given by people too insensitive to know they were being insulting if we should offer to come after them in our chariot. It would be an implication of interdependence, a suggestion that their way of life was less than whole. When they have arrived at our place we'll try our best to give them joy in horseback riding and in flying in a chariot behind horses at full gallop. I know they'll all love it and it will add to our enjoyment of each other. Someday we may each want to integrate some part of the other's way of life into our own pattern but we would no more want to be the same than a man and woman would want to be the same.

Although they have an enormous amount of leisure time most of the people at the lake travel around and meet others very little. However, they do conspicuously encourage others to visit them. In that way they try to keep up wide contacts. It's pretty generally believed that too much isolation may eventually run into cowardice — and possibly into pointless violence, born from an attempt to assure oneself that one is not a coward.

All the leisure of the lake people prompts them to make a great variety of non-essential things. Everywhere we went we would have been showered with gifts if we had expressed a liking that went beyond an appreciative curiosity. Here, no one but a very intimate friend will presume to give an uninvited gift. There were many highly imaginative and attractive baskets for various household purposes and containers of all sorts for carrying articles around. Also everyone had made a profusion of clever and beautiful clothing articles which they showed to us as examples of the fabricating methods they're developing. If I hadn't learned reticence in expressing my joy in these things, a sincere joy but often too enthusiastically expressed, I would have come back with a whole chariot full of things I would have trouble finding a use for. As it was I brought back only one thing, a blank book; I really wanted that and *I will use it*.

Two men who are neighbors have been working competitively for thirty years in developing a durable paper and unfading pen-pencil for permanent books. They compete in seclusion, then share each triumph of discovery. They now have something of which they are very proud. The paper is just a little heavy in my opinion but it does seem to be extremely durable. It is better than any paper made outside, but, what seems to be more important, it can be made simply. It can even be made in a sheet size tray by pouring equal amounts of two liquids together and picking up a precipitate

108

on a screen placed in the bottom of the tray. The precipitate can then either be dipped in a bath and rolled to make a hard glossy surface or left with a beautiful unshiny texture. None of the recipes are very complex and all the materials are easy to collect. At the same time these two also made up a binding that is substantial, easy to hold and write in, and easy to replace pages in loose leaf fashion. It is by far the best thing of its kind I have ever seen anywhere. But there is no use in describing it. I intend to have it the rest of my life and can show it to anyone.

19.

Writing about the book reminded me that I forgot to put down anything about the educational system after my first visit to Hans. This blank book is part of the same idea. *Restraint* in filling it will be the delayed beginning of my education.

The books in the library are all for research and are about ninety-five percent from the zombi world. Hans makes about ten percent of them freely available to anyone, about half to adults who are around twenty-five years old, and all to "anyone over fifty who has no better use for his time." But Hans makes it clear that his restrictions are only recommendations and he won't push them to the point of combat if anyone insists on looking at the books.

Zombi books dealing with plants and animals can often be used for research here without rewriting, as can some books on substance, like geology and astronomy. Chemistry and physics have to be rewritten completely. History and social studies as they are known in zombiland are, of course, not worth rewriting at all because most information of value was originally left out of them or interpreted from a zombi perspective. A complete work on "Retrogression of Homo sapiens" that is for general reference has been worked on by many for twenty years and Hans is the coordinator of the effort on that now. "People and Zombis," published 50 years ago, was a brief world history that was once used as a text book. Few use it any more; it was slightly vindictive. "A standard system of measuring by use of arbitraty hypothetical units" is a currently used text book that carries mathematics through algebra, geometry, and trigonometry. Most art is so cluttered with zombi meanings that it is valueless but some poetry and songs can be brought over intact, or with minor variations.

A goal of our development is the elimination of any need for published books. This is not because the publishing process is complicated but because mass produced books result in intellectual overeating and indigestion. Ultimately all books are expected to be hand produced.

The point of extremely durable paper and binding in loose leaf form is that each book is used continuously through one lifetime and, if it's good, kept for reference through several lifetimes. Each book is different because it's made by the individual who uses it. Ideally it contains the knowledge he has acquired, or hypotheses he made or accepted, which he thinks are worth preserving and passing on to others. There's much reworking of material and replacing of sheets, but there's an understandable personal pride in having sheets that date back to earliest childhood which have never had to be reworked.

The are no schools as I have known them. A common practice is for two to fifteen mothers and sometimes fathers, with children the same age, to join together and divide up the tedious chore of teaching their children "basic communication by arbitrary standards" — writing, reading, and measuring. Writing and reading are taught simultaneously and this is the only time work is expected to be thrown away immediately. For about two years the children write notes to each other. They have many squabbles, a natural tendency which I have been assured works out extremely well, over whether failure to communicate is bad writing or bad reading. The teacher is simply the referee and guide to staying within areas of what can be effectively communicated. The words of songs are the most commonly used material for reading practice of printed material. "People and Zombis" was used for a long time. A great variety of simple writings in disposable form on usually not more than four sheets of paper are available to anyone who wants them to familiarize the children with printed words.

Usually after two winters of practicing a child is ready to begin compiling his permanent books. He begins by making a dictionary and a book of measuring techniques. Luckily about sixty-five years ago a man with dreams saw the need for an arbitrator of communication standards and took on the job. The principles he laid down for future guidance were so sound that there's never been a disagreement that resulted in division. He chose English as the basic language but set up a standard of phonetic spellings. Also he made arbitrary choices between confusing word definitions. About sixty years ago Funk and Wagnalls proposed a system of phonetic spelling for zombiland but it apparently received little attention; I never heard of it. It was adopted here. The unabridged Funk and Wagnalls dictionaries circa 1920 are used as the arbitrary standard of phonetic spelling. Word definitions as set out in the dictionary are not accepted; the arbitrator had taken on the task of gradually cleaning up muddy definitions. Two successors have continued the cleaning up process. A child may find that the definition he has put in his book differs from that in his parents books. He thinks it is a great game to go to the arbitrary standard and see if the definition in his parents or his teacher's book has been modified, and all who are wrong must immediately make correction in their own books, and in their usage, if they are to hold his respect. So everyone is brought up to date along with the child.

Word definitions that are recognized as made by an arbitrator, instead of the dictionary trying to record common usage, serves another purpose. The distinction between standards of communication that require an arbitrator and the sort of knowledge where reality is the arbitrator is pointed up very sharply.

The metric system is the standard of measurement and the book on measuring begins with a description of the metric system's arbitrary creation. The fact that the metric system originated and is widely used in zombiland is pointed out. There is never any attempt to disclaim that the origin of a useful thing or a good idea is zombiland. Its history simply stops with the fact that it was "brought in." However in this case it is emphasized that the source of the arbitrary standard of measurement in now in zombiland and, if it ever becomes necessary to make extremely precise measurements, the desirability of checking and accepting the zombiland arbitrator's basic standards should be fully considered.

I have already learned that almost any twelve year old child here knows more mathematics than I do. Each has made his own text book and thoroughly understands principles that I accepted as dogma. I am going to have to learn something myself if I am going to carry my part of the teaching job when I have children. Fortunately for me mothers don't make a routine of trying to take the children beyond trigonometry in teaching them "measuring."

After the basics of communication are learned, usually before a child is ten years old, the phase of extending, selecting, organizing, and recording knowledge is begun. All of these facets have equal emphasis. One's books reflect personal preference and so become tangible pictures of one's personality.

Each person relies on his own judgment of what his books

shall be. Kirk is strong on selection and organization. Boleen has three times as much volume of books as he has, and Wang at least twice as much as Boleen. When I think of all the mountains of useless junk I put in notebooks and threw away during sixteen years of school it makes me shudder with shame.

With the mechanics of communication out of the way, the parents become fully aware that they're teaching their children as they go about their daily work together. Because they're not competing with anything similar to zombiland's state enforced authority of schools, and the enormous mass of non-essential information forced down the childrens' throats by schools, every child is hungry for knowledge. The healthy hunger for knowledge makes for a very relaxing and enjoyable relationship.

When the child begins organizing and writing down what he has learned he becomes thoughtful and incisive in his analysis. He comes up with questions and opinions. Teaching children gives way to a two way conversation from which both parents and children benefit.

Reality is accepted as the teacher. Biology is studied by actually controlling the growth of plants and animals for personal use. The field of chemistry is opened by analyzing the soil, by food preservation, and by tanning of leathers. Anatomy is studied when butchering cattle and preparing wild game for cooking.

It amazes me what an analytically intelligent, rather than a commercially expedient, approach to "farming" practices can do to change the sort of people involved in them. Here there are no farmers and workers raising the food for a "nation." Here there are individuals scientifically studying the art of living. As children, they study the mechanics of living as a novice painter studies materials and techniques before trying to become a master artist.

The education process exclusively between parents and their own children goes on for two or more years, depending on the parents and children. Thereafter formal education consists of attending open lectures or demonstrations covering many subjects. These are formalized by invitations announced by a file of cards that can be looked through in the library. Anyone who thinks he has something to offer puts a card on file stating the subject, scope, place (most often his home), limitation on number attending, and anything else he feels is pertinent. Cards are removed after two seasons and new ones have to be filled out if the announcement of the course is to continue. Considerable prestige is gained by offering a well attended course.

The variety of courses offered is unbelievable considering the limited number of people here. The social aspect is a very big factor, but I understand that prestige requires that one really have something to offer, and not "pad" the course just to prolong it. Most courses deal with extending knowledge of plants, animals, substances, and their possible uses. However some subjects would be unbelievable to zombiland educators who strive for "liberal education." I counted three cards offering courses in the techniques of love making by women to male classes of one. I asked one of the women who was working in the library about them and she said they disturbed no one. Sometimes attractive girls put cards like that in the file but mostly it's a last stand attemp to attract men, and after a look at a woman offering one, men usually decide she can't teach them much. One of the three, however, was pointed out to me as enjoying immense current popularity.

That's about all I remember now about the educational process but I want to get down an odd thought or two that came to me while I was writing.

As regards sexual promiscuity, many girls put up notices under lovers on the bulletin board that they'll accept all men. It has to mean just that. They can't bring a charge of rape against anyone under any conditions. There's a fair amount of unlimited promiscuity in sexual relations on this basis. The pressure of public opinion is generally against broad acceptance by women because most of the women who make them and most of the men who go to them seem to lack balance and fullness in their ways of life. But no one would think of trying to prohibit it other than by combat and it's usually not that important to anyone. Most of the women are sovereign but as long as they don't entice a man's young sons there is usually no trouble. If they do, the father has been known to challenge. I have been told that in most cases, unless the woman is completely lacking in desirability, a permanent or semipermanent relationship with one man usually develops and then there's a withdrawal of general acceptance.

Prostitution, usually spoken of as the oldest profession, isn't one here simply because there's no paid profession of any kind. There's no word for whore but sexual favors from women do come about as close to being something paid for as anything here. The women who drift into promiscuity usually do so because they have limited interests and they ask the men who visit them to bring them food and to do things around that need doing. The break-up most often comes because a man starts staying around the place working all the time and then grows jealous and drives off other men. Sometimes it goes on to formal combat, but the more usual thing is that only one man at a time thinks the woman is worth fighting over, and everyone else stays away when he stakes out his claim.

There is money, scrip, which can be used to buy things in the store but no one seems to value it. Buying and selling between individuals isn't a usual practice; also there's great pride in not buying things in the store. Everyone has money to burn and it is literally burned every year when new money is issued. I'm no economist but there's something here along that line that I don't fully understand yet. It has to do with the secret strategy in our relations to zombiland and talking about that is the one taboo everyone seems to respect. Kirk says he doesn't know it fully and he refuses to give me the incomplete information he does have. Everyone has the same attitude. No one is unkind about it but everyone is firm. I have learned that it's useless and bad taste to ask questions about it. I doubt that there is anything occult in the secret but I'll have to be patient.

That's about the only mystery surrounding this place that's left to me. I have become so good at astronomy that I can fix our latitude exactly and that narrows my guess of our location down to where I can be pretty sure about it.

The origin and history of Camp 38 is literally an open book. I've read much about it in the library and after I've cleared up another point or two for myself I plan to condense it into brief words as I would tell it to someone else — as I would tell it to Peggie if she should come here.

Peggie seems to belong to a world unbelievably far away and long ago. I was sort of her mother as well as her older sister and I have an old urge to look after her. I can think of nothing I'd rather do for her than bring her here. I can't imagine that she wouldn't like it. But she might not. I'm quite sure this place isn't the answer to everyone's dreams.

The whole history of the human species in the history of the man-made culture of zombis — of selectively breeding for zombi-ism. As the result of selective breeding, many are born zombis. Some willingly get drunk on zombiism. That leaves only an undetermined number who have zombiism thrust upon them. They are the only ones who want to escape.

114

The name Camp 38 doesn't date back to the year one. The name comes from a lumber camp that was set up here about ninety-six years ago. There have been clear factors of choice in bringing the people here together. The deliberate acts of two men, Hartman and Gilbert Durrell, were basic in setting the direction for our continuing society. I think a single deliberate act of Lin Tse could also be called basic. There were many contributing acts that an anthropologist would try to group, classify and call "forces." People here relate to "volition" more readily than they do to "forces." I can't measure the relative importance of the various volitions in reversing the tide of zombiism but I feel sure there must have been many thousands of cases like the initial action of Hartman that ended in a people who died aborning because there was no further impetus given at the critical moment.

The beginning story of Camp 38 has been written down by several persons and their original drafts are in the library. They're all in substantial agreement but some details differ. All are as told by the first couple here — a sort of Adam and Eve — who were still alive when the lumber camp was established. But only the major facts appear to be accurate. Details cannot be relied on. Because the man had killed under conditions that the zombi world would call "murder" he admittedly fabricated some of the details at the time he felt it was safe to tell his story and changed these details in various tellings. Many of the lumberjacks and most of the women left in Camp 38 had probably had trouble with the law and would take his side by natural inclination. Certainly, none of them, learning the man's story forty or fifty years later, made (or could have been expected to make) any attempt to pin down the facts to a point that would lead to a murder trial. The man was called Hartman and the woman who was the mother of his children was named Hilda but both names they admittedly made up and their original names were never known.

In the year one the broad area for a thousand kilometers surrounding here was inhabited primarily by Indians. A few white zombis had moved in but "they did not yet all respond to a common control."

Hartman was a well-built, strong nineteen year old boy coming west with his parents. (Sometimes the story is aunt and uncle, sometimes two brothers but the varieties are obviously smoke screens to hide facts that would identify him but have no other significance.) Either on a wagon train or at a new settlement (this is another point where the story varies greatly for the same obvious purpose) Hartman met Hilda who was then seventeen. On the occasion of their first meeting, or maybe soon afterwards, her cries brought him to her and he found an "old and ugly" man trying to "rape" her, slapping her about and upbraiding her for her sinfulness in defying the will of God who had given her to him in holy matrimony. Hartman had some unusual background that made him an atheist or agnostic and the old man evoking the name of his god to enforce his marriage prerogatives over his young wife added to the fury he already felt. He moved in on the man with his fists and ended up by killing him. Details differ as to method but in none of the stories did he claim self-defense. As an old, white-haired man he asserted that he intended to kill from the beginning — because he thought the man should be killed; he said he would do it again if he had the circumstances to live over.

Hartman and Hilda ran away together. Seeking a place of hiding from both the white zombis and the Indians, they finally made a permanent home here at the lake. Nothing is now left at the place they first lived but the spot is well-known. They lived in a sort of cave made by roofing over a rock walled crevice that was conveniently located by a creek. It was they who began the custom of burial trees for their dead and their own burial trees are still standing near the spot.

Survival apparently was never a problem. Also they were never disturbed either by those they had offended or by the Indians. Their problem was their aloneness and their wish for people. Hilda had been brought up to believe in the zombi gods but Hartman was able to calm her feeling of sinfulness that goes with that belief. However as they began to have children their concern, particularly Hilda's, was over what would happen to the children when they grew up. This concern occupied much of their thoughts.

Ignoring the world outside, they began their own calendar starting from their arrival here as the year one. They measured the shadows, kept an accurate day count, and embellished their count of time with four seasons. They discussed what they would teach their children about the world. Apparently Hartman was the leader in this and the things they decided on makes me wonder about his background; but nothing on that point is available. The children were taught that the world was full of sleep-walking zombis who couldn't be reasoned with. They were taught that the zombis claimed land they had never even seen and claimed that anyone who lived on the land automatically became one of them and was expected to take direction from a couple of imaginary beings — a god and a nation.

In the war between the whites and the Indians, Hartman favored the Indians, not because they were there first but because their claims to the land's possession were not based on any mumbo jumbo about god given property rights. Hartman and Hilda decided against teaching reading and writing to their children because these seemed useless abilities under the circumstances. Since they had decided to believe in no gods they were given to critical, and often incisive, ponderings over possible centers of volition in the inorganic world. This gave them something to talk about when they needed relief from the day to day concern with necessities.

Apparently Hartman and Hilda were extremely well-mated. Mates for their children were their only real problem. They constantly dreamed of finding a solution to this.

Hartman made extensive scouting trips as soon as the necessities of living were fairly well solved. On one of these he came upon an isolated cabin left in flames after an Indian raid. When the cabin had burned down and he felt sure no one was left he approached it to see if there were any remaining tools that he could take. In his crudely made skin clothes he may have been a puzzling sight, but a boy who had been hidden in the woods by his mother, recognized him as a white man and came running out, begging for his help.

There were four children hidden who had escaped the massacre, three boys and a girl, all under seven. The mother had been picking berries with them when the Indians struck, burned the house and killed her husband in the field. She was seen by the Indians when she made the mistake of hurrying too soon to her husband to see if he were still alive. One sent a parting arrow through her body.

The burned cabin was a full day's travel away from Hartman's home at the ground-covering speed at which he normally moved through the woods, and a very long way when he thought of taking the children with him. However he recognized that the solution to his primary problem had fallen into his hands and he had no intention of finding them some other foster home. He looked them all over carefully, decided they were good sturdy stock, and he was overjoyed. Three boys! He and Hilda had only one boy and one girl with another baby on the way. He said that at that moment he almost believed in all the stories of divine providence. The baby boy was still nursing but by chewing food and putting it into its mouth he managed to keep it nourished and, although it took him eight days, he brought all four children home with him and all lived.

There's no record as to whether the concept of incest disturbed the free thinking Hartman, but close inbreeding was never considered as a possible solution. However, with new blood in potential mates for his children he was not immediately concerned whether each had an individual mate. Boys, he had already decided, would not be a problem; they could go among the Indians and bring home with them Indian women who would be content with the life. Girls couldn't hope to bring home Indian braves. But with *three* unrelated men whom he and Hilda could raise up, all the girls might become mothers in their time and the next generation could interbreed as much as necessary.

And so it was. Eight living children and two that died were born to Hartman and Hilda. In all, the white group consisted of five girls and seven boys. A total of six Indian girls were brought home by the first generation of boys, eleven Indian girls were brought in by the next generation, and when the Camp 38 lumbering operation was opened here there was a total of fifty-eight persons of all ages living in and around the lake. Hartman and Hilda were apparently both of good physique and features and the boys who sought out Indian girls seemed to have had an eye for beauty. The earliest records often mention the attractiveness of the people.

Hartman made fairly frequent visits to keep informed on what was happening in the outside world as zombis settled the surrounding country. He took out furs and traded them for tools and rifles but he discouraged his children from going outside. It was only with great reluctance that he took one or two of the boys with him on some of his trips as they became men. Their acquaintance with the outside worked out the way he would have wanted it. After one of them served a month in jail "like an animal kept in a trap and fed" and "all for nothing but beating a man up in a fair fight" the horror of zombis who ganged up on people was brought home. The desired separation was easy for Hartman to maintain after that. Apparently total separation was a reasoned decision that became a prime objective with him.

Hartman was over sixty years old when Camp 38 was established. As the logging operation began to move up river in his direction he watched it apprehensively. By that time he and Hilda were fully joined in the wish to be left alone and to see their family of mixed white and Indian children grow into something better than either the whites or the Indians. They needed no one else. They were self-sufficient. They had forty year old fruit trees that as cuttings Hartman had carried into the hills. They had herds of cattle developed from a cow and a bull calf Hartman had brought through the woods forty years ago. They had fields they had cleared producing heavy grain and berries. They had domestic fowls and eggs. They didn't need the outside world and didn't want it.

Hartman knew the occasion of his killing a man would no longer be remembered and he and his progeny could all move into the newly developing settlements and be absorbed, or wait until the settlements moved to them. But he didn't want to see his family absorbed. His hatred of what he called the "white, pious, pompous, Bible-spouting zombis" was deep and he had instilled it in his children. To be made into a zombi was to them a fate worse than death and they watched the approach of the lumbering operation with that attitude. It was the approach of an enemy with whom there could be no terms for peace. And he knew that fighting zombis was more hopeless than fighting an invasion of millions of ants would have been if the ants were man size.

Hartman had seen the power of that white tide as it met the Indians. He never for a moment planned to fight it with the rifles he had brought in. He saw the mutilated land left by logging, and reasoned that his family might be able to survive the logging operation, as animals survived a forest fire. If they could it might give his family two or three generations to become a greater force before they finally had to deal with the zombi tide.

At first things went very smoothly. The new lumber camp was only a bunkhouse, mess hall, and supply station; there were no women. Several of Hartman's men took jobs as loggers and got along with the regular crew with no more fights than were usual among men of the varied types that followed logging work. The loggers got fresh milk, eggs, meat, and fruit from the lake settlement. The wages paid to Hartman's men were less than half paid to the others and food was bought delivered to the camp kitchen at much less than the price that would have been paid outside. The long haul in was spared and the variety and freshness of the food made the workmen happy. Also the beginning of relationships developed between the men at the camp and the girls at the lake with no difficulty the first year.

The foreman and loggers got a percentage of profits as part of their wages but they were part of an already big lumber producing company, owned and run by one man, H. J. Durrell. Like all who push into new areas he was a personal empire builder and a man of quick decisions. Impressed by the run and the profits the first year after the camp was established, he made a personal visit to find out what had caused the better than usual success. What he found pleased him. Doubtless he considered that he owned the land used by Hartman but a source of food in the remote place and a source of cheap labor far outweighed the value of a few acres of land remote from any settlement. He never mentioned ownership. He dealt in immediate realities. He needed a permanent camp as a basis for logging this area and he made Camp 38 into a basic supply center. He brought in saw mill equipment, built some flimsy houses for loggers with families and set up a company store.

The next two or three years the logs continued to flow. However friction began developing between the families of the men who settled and what they called the "ungodly, degenerate whites and red heathens" at the lake. But "H. J.," as he was called, had made a decision and had begun acting on it. He imported two families of Chinese and settled them on the level land on the south shore of the lake to raise produce as Hartman was doing. Then he left the seed he had planted. He had many things going in his empire and didn't get back to Camp 38 for two years.

Fights didn't become more frequent at the camp but they became more serious. Axes, knives, and rifles began to take the place of fists. It isn't practical for a logger to wear a gun and the foreman made a rule against carrying small arms in the pockets while at work but a man wearing a gun off duty came to be a common sight. There were killings and visits by the sheriff, resulting in trials outside and at least one hanging. Except for some white men who had Indian wives and who found easy acceptance of "squaw men" here, most men with families didn't stay more than one season. Some of the houses began to stand vacant. Several of Hartman's progeny who were working as loggers moved into the camp houses with their women and children, and some of the single loggers lived with Hartman's girls in the family houses.

The word marriage could clearly not be used in describing the relationships between any of Hartman's offspring. That was the major cause of the friction when the families began to move in, and that was the fact that H. J. had not known when he decided to make use of the cheap labor. Marriage and a man's "respectable rights" over a woman were among the things Hartman had taught his people to look upon as the foul practices of the zombis.

Just before the first year's spring run of logs the story of the native people's attitude toward marriage got back to the lumber camp but it wasn't fully believed. It sounded like another logging camp joke. One of the loggers who had got a young girl at the lake pregnant offered to take her out after the run and marry her. She went into a rage, beat and scratched, and was so insulted that she ran away and wouldn't speak or have anything more to do with him. He had to learn from others what was the matter with her.

When he told the story at the camp that the people here believed marriage was a slave contract and had no rules of love making but that sexual relations were always woman's choice he was laughed at for walking in his dreams, called a zombi — a word that had been picked up and used jokingly by the loggers — and accused of having a secret supply of opium. Then other men, whose experience had made them wonder about it but who had never offered the supreme insult of marriage to any of the girls, added what they had learned.

However the incredible story was not filled in fully until next season. Then there were married men with their families living right alongside the people who had been imbued with Hartman's hatred of marriage. One of the pillars of zombi society was threatened and Hartman's offspring had an opportunity to see for themselves how zombis behave under such circumstances.

The other major principle that Hartman had instilled in his family was all that avoided a quick decisive conflagration. This was the principle that all "fair fights" had a single criterion — one man against one man on an equal basis. When the friction developed, Hartman's men refused to become a solid front in defense of one of their own. Their attitude when one of their blood got into trouble was "hands off, it's his fight, but it has to be a fair fight."

The loggers understood and rallied to the cry of fair fight. When the fights became more serious they were willing to approve fair fights with knives and axes arranged away from the women and certain of the men in the camp. All felt honor bound to stick to a story that the wounds or death of the loser was accidental. But when guns came into play and a fair fight came to be considered as two men approaching each other with rifles from opposite sides of a designated timber area, the gun shot wounds and deaths were harder to call accidental. After a few experiences with the sheriff, and after a crack pistol shot came in and insisted that a fair fight was two men in the open walking toward each other with guns on their hips, they all agreed that fights thereafter must either be "friendly" with fists or "to the death" with knives and axes. This became a basic practice that served to draw the men together.

However, no basis for reconciling marriage and the rule that sexual relations were simply woman's choice was ever reached. Most of the loggers found Hartman's teachings eminently acceptable but their wives did not. Formal-looking notices of the girls' acceptance of lovers, with art borders like marriage licenses, were prepared and put on the bulletin board in the company office on several occasions. But these infuriated those who upheld the holiness of matrimony much more than they pacified them.

The next visit by H. J. to see why his first plans hadn't worked out brought another decisive change to Camp 38. He weighed the assets and decided the hard-working, low-wage natives, who spent all those low wages at the company store, were valuable enough to warrant some concessions to their idiosyncrasies. He admitted to the protesting family men that Hartman's people were all "half-Indian heathens" but proclaimed that he was no missionary. He made satisfactory agreements whereby the men with families could leave if they wanted to do so and made a policy of bringing in no further families unless they fully understood what they were getting into and, like the "squaw men," might like it there. He saw that the Chinese families were taking over more of the food raising and freeing Hartman's men for lumbering. This looked to him like a good trend, so he went back to San Francisco and sent out another Chinese family.

Since he was now going to put emphasis on making a permanent camp primarily out of single men, he made some arrangement with a madam in a San Francisco brothel to send up some girls with temperaments fitted to the place. From time to time a total of about fifteen of these girls came in but they didn't work out well; they either got bored and left or attached themselves to one man and settled down. However for awhile a brothel at Camp 38 did do enough business to make it worthwhile for the girls to stay.

During its course an incident occurred that put the Chinese strongly behind a practice that Hartman had been working to formalize. Hartman wanted everyone to agree to a local trial and execution of anyone guilty of rape. Rape was to be determined by failure to have the girls choice entered in a register kept in the company office. Since the girls couldn't write and the loggers couldn't be trusted in such a matter, the handwriting of Hartman or Hilda only was to be accepted. He made it clear that this was not to be a taken as "giving in marriage" but simply authenticating the girl's choice.

The Chinese had their own concepts of marriage and felt strongly about them. One of the first families sent back to China for a bride who had been promised to one of their boys when he was a baby. She arrived at the camp in due time but something went wrong with the aid H. J. was giving in the case and she ended up in the brothel. Her protestations were inarticulate and when word of her arrival reached her betrothed and he came for her she was already slightly shopworn. The Chinese thereafter took more interest in Hartman's concept of woman's choice in the matter of lovers and also in the Hartman taught concept of a fair fight. This had now taken a standard form of two men meeting in an area in the woods with either knives or axes — no rules and no witnesses.

After their interest had been aroused, the Chinese came into a full participation by a single incident. The incident also added a significant item to what was developing into a standard form of agreement.

An enormously big lumberjack, who was also a bully, took a delight in tormenting the Chinese whenever they appeared at the company store. He thought it especially hillarious to trip them when they were loaded with supplies and going out the door. Also he kept alive and continually embellished the mistake of the intended bride being placed in the brothel. His joy in that joke on these small stature people, when his only pride was his bulk and strength, reached to inexhaustible extremes. The hatred that the Chinese felt for him is fully understandable when the stories told show that the other loggers were ashamed that he was one of them. The Chinese had become well enough acquainted with the logger's ways to understand most of the foul jokes and to understand that this man's attitude didn't represent that held by most of the others. The other loggers continually admonished the bully with "you wouldn't talk like that to a man who was big enough to challenge you to a fight."

Then one day when this remark was made after the usual taunts from the giant logger it brought a memorable response from one of the Chinese. The target at the moment was a slight, sensitive-faced Chinese man named Lin Tse who had come into the store

123

alone. The fury that had been burning showed itself in this man who contained it with the patient endurance that countless centuries had bred in his being. It didn't leap into flame; it glowed with a small controlled dignity like some unearthly fire.

Lin's purchase was only a small package and although there was a big audience of men gathered in the store the bully didn't think it worthwhile to trip him as he went out. He contented himself with foul worded jokes. Lin heard the other loggers disapproval expressed in "you'd be more careful with a man who was big enough to fight you." Lin Tse knew the full meaning of the fight to which the words referred and his understanding and deliberation created drama when he turned and faced the bully and the roomful of men with dignity.

The surprise of his turning to meet them instead of hurrying out the door as unobtrusively as possible caused a hush to fall. In the waiting silence his words were clear and in fully understandable English, "If you gentlemen will insure a fair fight, I will meet this man."

There was only a short pause before someone said enthusiastically, "Let's give them guns. That's the only way to make a fair fight in this case."

The foreman was there and spoke up. "No. We've all agreed. No more guns. I'd like to see the little guy have his chance, but the judge said if there's another suspicious shooting every man here will face trial as an accomplice of a murderer.

Before an argument developed on the point Lin announced, "I do not want guns. Fifteen meters of strong cordage in addition to a knife will make an equal fight if there's a big area that has not been logged clean."

The big man didn't like the sound of things and, with a guffaw, he tried to go back to the joking game, "He wants to tie me up before he fights me." He pulled the end of rope from a nearby coil, threw it at Lin, and held out his wrists with, "Here, let's see you do it."

No one laughed. The men were all on their feet and approaching the little man with an interest that was clearly that of a wolf pack moving up on a fight, but also with a silence that verged on becoming a reverent calm. They asked what he could do with a length of cordage.

Lin answered, "Man is intelligent. His intelligence makes him a fit opponent for a bear or even an elephant. With a knife and a cord a man can make a spear, or a bow and arrow, or a trap. He

124

can do many things. He can fight with his intelligence, not just his bulk or his skill in handling a gun. But surprise is necessary to use intelligence. Man does not show the bear how he plans to trap him. I think it is fair that I and this man-bear have equal knives and lengths of cord but do not tell how we will use them."

The trap had been sprung. A man had used the weight of a mob for an intelligent purpose by appealing to fair play rather than the usual half-sleeping mob tendencies toward turning a fight into mob entertainment. The bully tried all the jokes and tricks he had learned in his attempt to put a laughing, leering mob behind him, but the mob weight was all used to make him accept the challenge on the fair terms stated. He wanted to reduce the size of the combat area but they insisted on making it big enough to give strategy its due weight.

The fight lasted a day and a night and well into the next day. Three times the big man tried to come out but the jeers of the others drove him back. At twilight on the second day, when everyone was preparing to go into another all night vigil, Lin appeared at the designated place and said calmly, "A man is dead in the woods. Would some of you gentlemen help me carry him out."

If the method Lin used to bring down the big man was ever known, it isn't of record, but the occasion touched the imagination of the men. An area big enough to permit strategy, a knife with a 25 cm. blade, too short for sophisticated swordsmanship, and a fifteen meter length of cordage, strong enough to jerk up a big man's weight, became the criteria of a fair fight.

Whether it was: (1) Simple fear of the unknown when contemplated through light and dark hours in the forest or (2) a new respect for the unknown in people, when meeting those different from oneself; would be hard to determine; but the number of deaths by unstated causes in Camp 38 decreased after the establishment of those criteria for fairness.

22.

For the next two years everything at Camp 38 went very smoothly. The register of women's acceptance and withdrawal of acceptances at the company office became a standard thing. An occasional Chinese name appeared in it. Cooperation between the white and Indian people and the Chinese at the lake became commonplace and fully evident.

If H. J. had returned he would have been pleased. But he died while visiting one of the other camps. After a few months his son came to the camp for a visit in the course of looking over his inheritance. But Camp 38 was an insignificant part of the big holdings and he didn't stay long.

Later he apparently heard some stories that gave him more interest in the camp than what he had seen. A little over a year after his first visit he came back, took one of the houses and had it made comfortable enough for an extended visit.

Gilbert Durrell was categorized by the loggers as "born with a silver spoon in his mouth." But a life of luxury is sometimes not without its own hardships. Luxury often gives rise to an environment of undisciplined personalities that is much more difficult to face than the hardships of a natural environment. Gilbert must have been born in some such environment. He was not the arrogant, young, inexperienced, college boy that the men had expected when they heard that the boss's son was coming out to take over. He was clean-shaven, his clothes had been pressed, and his hands had no calluses; but he was thirty years old and something in his face said his life had put pressures on him and he had done his own fighting against those pressures. He hadn't won but he had survived. Like an animal who has met men and guns and traps and come away from numerous close encounters without being maimed, his movements suggested a knowledge of powerful opposing forces and a will to meet them with his full ability and a watchful eye. Although not a big man by logger's standards he was above average in height and moved as if he could make full use of his weight. Resentment against the power of the wealth he had at his command could not be effaced, but otherwise the loggers recognized him as being a man by their standards.

When he came back the second time, his obvious intention to stay around awhile made everyone uneasy, but he didn't try to be a regular fellow and show he could do rough and dangerous work with the best of them — his attitude always acknowledged his unique position. After several days they were able to accept him for what he was.

As they later learned he had no children but had been married and divorced. There's a record of his education which included several colleges in the United States and Europe with special interests in law, history, and philosophy but there's nothing on the cause of his divorce. All that's known is that it apparently left him with little interest in women. The girls at that time often moved about the camp scantily clad in skins and the men remarked that he could watch them with the same measuring but uninvolved eye that he turned on horses and dogs.

However he seemed to like both horses and dogs in a detached sort of way and he also gradually showed some interest in the girls. Even as he would often start, or respond to, a conversation with the men that had no bearing on the work so, also, he could often be seen in conversation with the women and girls in the store or somewhere about the camp.

He visited Hartman at his place, which at that time was still half cave, and showed his interest by repeated and often lengthy stays. Hilda and her attitude toward the life she had lived particularly interested him.

He also spent a great deal of time with the Chinese families and wanted to know how they had come to accept some matings between their own and Hartman's families when there were no elaborate Chinese marriage ceremonies. The answer that they did it because it was the custom in this country seemed to open a field of thought for him that he wanted to pursue. On his first trip out, after staying at the camp five weeks, he brought back two books on marriage customs and one exclusively on Chinese marriages. He also brought back a great number of other books as if he intended to spend considerable time here.

He did stay from late fall until early spring on that trip. How much it was preplanned and how much it was a new interest that he found here isn't known. But on that trip a sixteen year old girl named Walona came to occupy a good deal of his time. She was one of Hartman's granddaughters and as nearly as I can follow the names, which often repeat next generation, she was three eighths Indian — a poised and beautiful girl.

He talked to her several times in the store about what she enjoyed and whether she was interested in the world outside. She expressed a strong horror of the outside and said she had already seen enough of what it was like from the people who came in. Apparently his attention to her was not deliberate courtship but he asked her to go in the company office with him several times and sit down where they could talk at length. She did so with good grace and everyone who overheard parts of the conversation said there was never anything to lead the girl to think he had any romantic interest in her. However, she had an acceptance of him as her lover written down in the company office register.

It was several days before he was aware of it. The men made

some jokes about it and one of them mentioned to Gilbert that if that little girl had made an acceptance of him he wouldn't be spending his nights alone. It was several days after that before Gilbert asked Walona to his house rather than the office for the talks that had become routine between them, and even longer before she spent the first night with him and later moved in. In the early spring he left the camp and returned late in the summer. Meanwhile she continued to live in his house.

While he was gone the camp lost a great number of men and also lost the three remaining whores who were keeping an open brothel. Gold had been discovered in Alaska and the lure of gold and far off places was more than most of the single unattached loggers could resist. Logging was on a greatly reduced scale that winter but all the land around the camp and lake had already been logged and there was no pressure on the camp.

Hartman took advantage of the lull in zombi activity to push in the direction his people wanted to go. He had often talked to Gilbert about his dream of making formal recorded agreements on the basis of the practices here. Now Gilbert had full time to give to Hartman's ideas; and he had the knowledge and ability to put them on a working basis. He helped Hartman draw up the form of agreement as it now stands.

After about a year, during which Gilbert quietly transferred those to whom he knew the agreements would be unacceptable to other camps, all remaining at Camp 38 formally entered into the agreements. This was a total of 347 persons.

Gilbert apparently was too complicated a man for others to analyze and leave a sound record of, and he left no writings of his personal history himself. He continued to come and go from the camp but spent an increasing amount of time here. All his life he continued to live with Walona but they never had any children. He died from a bad heart when she was only twenty-six and she later accepted another man and had three children. The other man, Duncan Hull, was a man of about Gilbert's age, whom he had known on the outside and brought here about six years before his death.

After the agreements had been signed, Gilbert brought in a total of five persons from the outside who lived here the rest of their lives. Except for Duncan all were around sixty years of age or older and only one left any children. Two were women and three were men. They did the initial work on modifying the language used here and giving form to the educational system that is now used.

Obviously Gilbert chose them because he knew they would nourish the culture of natural individual sovereignty that had originated in the solitude of Hartman and Hilda. Apparently he chose them with keen perception. Their motivation seemed to be the reverse of missionaries. Instead of imposing an outside culture on the people here, they concentrated on helping the people here recognize precisely what they wanted to reject in the outside culture, and what they must do to keep the outside from intruding on them.

Gilbert originally undertook the task of keeping the camp completely isolated from the rest of the world. The logging operations were stopped and all the other camps were closed within about three years after the formal agreement between everyone here. The roads to the outside were soon closed completely.

Just how total isolation is now accomplished is far from clear to me. Although there is now a network of chariot roads, they apparently don't extend to our boundaries. I know that Kirk and I came in on a horse trail where we had to ride single file most of the way. Presumably all this land was owned by Gilbert and was deeded to someone here, maybe to the Camp 38 company, which is the name on the scrip used for money.

This is again valuable timber land and someone must be paying taxes on it. Possibly a trust fund. No one volunteers information on the subject and I get the feeling that prying into it would be very poor taste for someone as new here as I am.

I would be willing to accept it all without question if I were sure that we won't come into full contact with the outside at any moment with catastrophic results for us all. I keep wondering. But Hans doubtless knows everything and he doesn't seem to worry; Kirk knows more than I and he doesn't worry. I suppose I will find out in time and meanwhile I should accept the here and now.

23.

Here there are no churches, no political rallies, no spectator sports, no school colors and cheer leaders, no radio, no television and no newspapers. It is a world of green forests, little fields, hidden houses, individual human beings, horses, dogs, and wild animals — all known intimately as personalities. Ordinarily discrete entities dissolve into an emotional oneness only when Nature rises to dominance, when there is a rising wind, a blowing rain; or when, on warm moonlit nights, the infinitely numerous small sounds blend into a universal chorus.

In the bright sunshine of warm summer days each living thing is an entity separate and distinct, a thing to be heard, smelled, tasted, seen, handled, and known for itself alone.

That other world, where one is constantly aware of tangible, man-made bonds uniting people, had ceased to exist for me. Then I felt something stir in the attitude of the people I met that reminded me of it.

It came with the mention of the open air "opera." I had been to Hollywood Bowl and an outdoor performance of an Indian play at Mount Tamalpais but it was not the memory of the crowds and bustling activity of these similar events that the talk of the coming outdoor performance evoked. It was something deeper and more significant. I felt a tingle like an electric charge running through all the people and bringing them together. It was primeval. It made me think of a wolf-call on a distant hill, an answering call nearer, another, another, a chorus, a pack.

But it was not something I heard from the detached perspective of a human being listening to the cries of wolves in the night; it was not a cold chill that ran up my spine and a concern for my own safety. This that I felt in others aroused also a note of response in me. It was like the feeling that goes through that other world when suddenly on everyone's lips is heard the ominous news that an enemy has invaded, that war had been declared. There was a sense of drawing close to friends so as to consult on strategy for defense against an invading enemy. "Only three more days 'till the opera. I hope the good weather holds." Intuitively I felt it. It puzzled my logical reasoning.

I went to the library and read the original libretto of Wagner's Ring operas and I was more puzzled. I could make nothing of them. I learned that they were based upon the religion or cultural concepts of the Northern Europeans before theocracy. But I also learned that the old songs that had carried this on had been deliberately mutilated by the organized effort of theocratic monks who worked them over for several centuries until no meaning was left in the juxtaposed and distorted conglomerate. Wagner had created anew.

Seeking a straw, my mind grasped at the suggestion that what I was feeling was a primeval cry in the night that was once significant to a people now gone. I equated it with the cry of an ancestral wolf pack heard in the dreams of a domestic dog sleeping by the fireside. I thought it might be the stirring of my Northern European ancestry within me. It seemed to bring on a heightened intensity of being.

As the first night of the four night series of operas approached, the feeling was stronger than ever. I somehow felt that I was preparing for a great experience.

At Kirk's suggestion I wore suede leather. It seemed to me appropriate for an outdoor theater. To my surprise he also dressed carefully in leather. I had not yet come to terms with the fact that he was dressing in leather when he topped it off by putting on a wide belt and a short sword. Then as a still further touch in the same spirit he brought out a present for me — a silver replica of the sword he was wearing with his name lettered on it in gold. He pinned it horizontally on my suede dress over the left breast. Such a pin Margaret had worn at my acceptance party and Dag had worn such a sword as Kirk's. Kirk explained that a sword is the mark of a sovereign. The pin indicates the sovereign by whom one is shielded. The name is one's sword-name. (The thought passed through my head that sword-name was the original term and surname a corruption. But I did not think that was a good time to pursue the idea. The mood of emotional charge was still building.)

When we arrived and I had a chance to look around, I saw that leather appeared to be formal dress for the opera, at least for men. Almost all men were dressed in leather. Most of the women were also, although among the women, there was a conspicuous sprinkling of exceptions. Everyone either wore a sword or a pin with the name of one's sovereign on it. There were no exceptions to this. Even the children wore pins. I noticed a small baby carried in its mother's arms with one on. I had not been wrong. Everyone was responding fully to what I began to think of as a battle cry. And there were more people than I had thought those wooded hills and valleys contained.

For the amphitheater a place had been chosen in a small bowl-like valley that provided fully adequate seating on symetrically arranged split logs for the two or three thousand there. There were no artificial lights. In the moonlight a large smooth stage floor with what looked like several big rocks on it was barely visible. It could almost have passed unnoticed among the trees. I supposed that there must be dressing rooms and some performance mechanism but if so the trees screened everything completely. People talked quietly, the stillness of the night was bigger than the sound of their voices.

I looked about wondering how the people here felt when this

131

was probably the only performance of any kind they ever witnessed. It was the sort of thing that practically fills the lives of people as I had known them up to a few months ago, but here it comes only once a year. I would have thought it would be a big event mostly by reason of its uniqueness. However, in the conversations that I overheard the content of the coming performance seemed to be everything; the novel experience of having a performance at all seemed to impress only the very young.

In college the general attitude was that every opera was a bore and those who were conversant enough to discriminate said Wagner's operas were the biggest bore of all. I had never seen any of the Ring operas performed. Kirk had warned me that what I was going to see was not really opera; there aren't enough high quality voices here; most of the words would be spoken. I expected that afterward I would need to watch myself in walking a tightrope between being patronizingly insincere and hurting someone's feelings. But mostly I was puzzled and curious. Perhaps no one was more eager than I for the first notes or words, whatever was to come. I waited quietly and didn't talk.

Then a low incessant pulse of sound filled the air. It didn't come from anywhere and it came from everywhere. The people's voices quieted as they listened. The sound filled the bowl slowly and possessed the people. They gave themselves to it freely. Then it rose on to possess the night. The voices of the night gave over to the sounds. The rhythmic sound took full command of everyone's hearing. Then everyone's vision was also captured.

Down among the trees at the stage a faint glow of dawn appeared to be breaking. As the dawn came on the roll of ocean waves became visible. Apparently a slowly lighting movie film shown on a backdrop screen made up much of the stage scenery. What had looked like a stage with rocks became an ocean beach and the trees of the little bowl in which we were sitting grew down to the beach. What we were seeing was reality and we were all part of the whole.

Bingee was playing on the rocks. She was wearing a leather sunsuit, the same or one very similar to that in which I had first seen her in the fields. Her feet appeared to be bare but I could tell from her movements as she played at the edge of the waves that she was wearing skin colored ballet slippers. She ran and danced and played in the waves. She held out her arms to the ocean as she danced; her motions were at first playfully enticing and then the motions of one offering her sincere love. She was making love to

132

each wave from the ocean as each rolled in only to dissolve in her arms.

From on top of a rock where she had been stretched out unseen, Lolena sat up and called to Bingee, asking if she were watching the ocean to be sure that no one would take it away. Her tone was half playful, half serious. A little later Inger also appeared and all three played and danced on the beach together.

The meaning of their ballet was enjoyment of the world as it is. Their words questioned the meaning of Wotan's warning to let no one take from them the wildgold — the ocean, the mountains, the sun, and the stars.

All were wearing leather sunsuits and invisible ballet shoes that made them part of the natural scene. An unattractive man in thick spectacles and conspicuous swim suit came onto the beach and called out that he was taking a vacation and wanted to join them. As he was clearly different from their kind, they immediately suspected that he might be one of those who, by some subtle trickery, are able to take from people the ocean and the woods, maybe even the sun and the moon and the stars.

I was caught up in the naturalness so completely that I didn't begin to notice quality until I heard the voice of the dwarf, which was as deliberately discordant as his clothes. The girls had seemed so familiar to me, had spoken in so much their regular voices, and behaved in so much their regular manner that I almost forgot they were acting. The sound system was so good that it passed unnoticed. The music was obviously recorded outside as there is no orchestra here capable of a quality as high as that.

The entire first scene was a ballet performed on the seashore. At first the dwarf ludicrously attempted to join the girls in their play. They laughed at his efforts and agreed among themselves that he couldn't be the sort of enemy against whom Wotan had warned — an enemy who knew nothing of love — because his behavior was that of a lovesick frog. Eventually they got tired of making sport of him and went back to their simple enjoyment of the waves and sand and the wind in the trees.

Being ignored made him furious. He followed them, while trying to get their attention by ridiculing them for being content with the cold dirty water when they could be enjoying all the wealth that can be made from the ocean and the rocks and the woods. They let him know they knew all about the things which the dwarfs made. They added that they were also fully aware of the power dwarfs could gain by dangling wealth before the eyes of

133

people who were fond of such things. But they laughed at him for thinking such a lovesick frog as he could do it. They told him that in order to mold and manipulate that kind of power one had to spend all his time on it, had to give up everything else — even had to forswear love.

"Does one who values love higher than power carry around as pocket trinkets such wealth as this?" he asked, throwing a long glittering neckless on the beach. "Take that," he said as he swaggered off, "and know that I can offer mountains more that will make this look dowdy by comparison."

By this gesture they recognized him as one of those against whom Wotan had warned — those who take by stealth while distracting their victims by continually giving them gifts.

All the wildsmaidens backed away from the necklace. Then Lolena came back, picked it up gingerly, and examined it tentatively. Bingee and Inger came up and all examined it with increasing interest. Becoming bolder they ran its heavy links through their fingers and held it up to the light. Then Inger suddenly seized it and threw it toward the surf.

All three stood staring at the glittering thing on the sand in indecision then, as a wave threatened to cover it, Lolena rushed forward and grabbed it up. She examined it again hesitatingly for a moment, then admiringly wound it around her wrist and danced about. After a while she tried it about her waist and danced again then, at last, about her neck as she continued dancing. Meanwhile Bingee and Inger watched, first in horror, then in interest, and at last approached and watched with envy.

The scene grew dark and I was again looking at the little moonlit valley. There was silence. A low murmur of voices gradually began but no one had cheered. For a moment I wondered if the absence of cheering was what accounted for the feeling I had. But much more was involved. What I was experiencing was a face to face meeting with the feeling that had permeated the people as this night approached. I realized that sitting quietly in an audience together we were all watching something of vital importance to us. This was not merely entertainment for people who, by passing up a profusion of entertainment as I had known it, could appreciate what they were now offered as a man lost in a desert can appreciate water. This was not an audience being entertained. There was nothing comparable to it in my past experience. This was both intellectual perception and the emotional experience of dream, religion, art in all its forms, politics — every manner of looking at life —brought into focus with a clarity that no single facet could give. In that first scene the theme of the coming four nights of "opera" had been stated. That theme was also a full statement of the actual relations between this little group of people watching attentively and the immense zombiland that surrounds us. What impressed me was that the relationship had been articulated with both a reasoned and an emotional clarity that I would have thought impossible for a relationship so complex.

No suggestion of this had come to me as I had read the original libretto. The meaningfulness came because I had become one of the people whose own thoughts and emotions were projected before our eyes and ears in absolute fidelity. My change of perspective to that of this audience was the thing responsible for bringing my empathy for the opera into focus — not merely the slight changes in the art form. These form changes were simple mechanical ones; from opera to ballet-drama, from the waters of the Rhine to the sands of an anonymous beach, and so on. There were also some translations from one symbol to another that spoke more clearly to the current audience. But essence was unaltered.

I tried to imagine how the next scene could possibly sustain that first absolute communion between an artist in another time and place and the people here and now. Going over in my mind the libretto as I had read it, I could not. But when the music asked for attention and the lights drew my eyes back to the stage again, I saw the same clarity again and had to believe that it could continue for four nights.

It was Wagner's music again and even most of his words were preserved but the new audience perspective, and some slight changes in language and symbols, brought on *total* understanding. I feel sure that what he brought to the people here had an eloquence that no other audience has ever appreciated.

As Wagner had written it the next scene was a hillside and Wotan was waking from a dream. Here the scene was transferred to the rough-hewn living room of Wotan's home and military headquarters. Through the window could be seen Valhalla, a city of spendor as great as any in the zombi world. The room was Camp 38; the city seen through the window was the world outside. The voice of understandable symbolism spoke clearly in Wotan's dress: he wore leather and a short sword as did most of the men in the audience.

When the opera had first been performed a commonplace native reality of dress had been put on the stage and the clarity of what it said in art had been adopted as a real life formality. Now life and art were one. Fricka wore a cloth dress. Then I noticed that she wore no pin with a sword name on it. I understood completely. This clearly alienated her. I remembered that she was the goddess of contractual marriage.

The scene still followed the original libretto except for an occasional phrase. The slight changes made it clear that Fricka and Wotan had made fateful compromises to gain Valhalla. They had both followed the motif stated by the wildsmaidens. Both had overstepped prudence in their eagerness to get what the dwarfs could offer. Fricka had fully embraced the concept of marriage. Wotan wanted power; however Valhalla — the sterile, shining but empty symbol of power, seen through the window — was what he actually got. The same thing, as an empty symbol of prestige, was all Fricka had to show for her attempts to find security in contractual marriage.

. . . I don't want to get carried away and describe all four operas. That would mean much too much writing. During four beautiful moonlit nights we looked at many possibilities under which people here might try to come to terms with the zombi world. The consequences of each possibility, when played out to its inevitable conclusion, showed that every one would result in tragedy.

What was depicted in the operas was not the relations between the people here and now and the zombi world as that relation would be if we now related. Under present realities there would be no drama. If our worlds came together now, we would be totally destroyed with no more drama than would be apparent if one of the big zombi wheat combines should pass over a nest of meadowlarks.

Now we are a few people in a big zombi world and, understandably, our present objective is to be left alone. But if the people here grow in numbers and if the outside zombis should be reduced in numbers, from either atomic war or from loss of joy in living, then there might be an approach to balance between us. *Then* we might think something could be gained by coming to terms. Then a Wotan might try to lead the people here into making some treaty with the establishment. It was that possibility that the opera considered and cried out against.

In the four nights many possible contacts between us and the outside world were considered. There was the story of Siegmund and Sieglinde living among dwarfs without knowing their god heredity. There was the story of Siegfried in the same circumstance awakened to his heredity and then being tricked into a pledge of brotherhood with the dwarf's offspring. There was the story of Brunnhilde whom Wotan, in faithfulness to his contracts with dwarfs, abandoned. She was awakened to full knowledge of her godhood, only to be betrayed by Siegfried's forgetfulness. On and on the many possibilities were dramatized in the intricately interwoven fabric of the story.

All the situations of the entire portrayal were real possibilities of what we may face in the future. And that future is widely recognized as being near enough so that we need to consider these dangers now.

I believe that no one here would argue against the accuracy of any cause and effect patterns presented in all the four nights. But for all the variety presented those four operas don't come close to exhausting the subject. They merely give a language in which to talk about it.

Ordinarily no one mentions the zombi world here because it is well-known that the delicate barrier that separates it from us is penetrated and made less a barrier by each careless word. But the Ring operas are a completely self-contained world in which we can see ourselves in possible relation to the zombi world. The virtue is that in the operas we see the situation objectively and without danger of upsetting a separation that is dependent on the delicate barrier stated by the words "we don't relate."

Everything about the zombi world is depicted in the four operas as they are staged here: Automobiles, airplanes; all forms of warfare from cold steel to atomic bombs; radio, television, telephones, intercoms; parades, department stores; labor unions, theocracies, political manipulation; the surreptitious control of public opinion in television and movies; the secret ballot as a concept, and the manipulation of the secret ballot for covert purposes.

Since everything is there, and an objective viewpoint is maintained, it can all be discussed without relating to the current zombi world. All the children see and know that what they are seeing is something real. The operas emphasize that *any* treaty with those of the opposing culture, *even if we should someday become more powerful than they,* can only end in our own destruction. Perpetuating this message carried by the operas is an all important social undertaking. Everyone here is aware of this.

During the days enveloping the operas there was an orgy of discussion on our relationship with the outside. I found that I could talk to anyone. Acceptable conversation is all a matter of not becoming involved in the day to day problems of the zombi world. The language cannot be the United States, Russia, or California. It must be Fasolt, Fafner,or Nibelungenland.

I must confess that, when deprived of the atmosphere of proudly parroting inconsequential facts, as I came to do in school, I, at first, had very little to say. Even though I had majored in anthropology, I had never thought about the world into which I had been born in an intellectual manner. I had never thought about it without prejudices and predilections. Like everyone else I had accepted the current world as a norm, an absolute, a thing by which to measure, not a thing to be measured.

But as the orgies of word discussions continued, silenced four times by evenings that said more than words alone can say, I came to feel in my blood and bone the thing I had sensed even before the first opening night. It has now become a conscious part of me.

The something to which I had instinctively responded was not quite like the cry of the wolf pack. Certainly it was not at all like the conversational buzz that characterizes the response of zombis to a surprise bombing. Here there is neither wolf cry, nor a savage beating of drums accompanied by military marches and flag waving. This is something different from hunting with the pack, different from animal self-protection, and different from war between those engaged in a game that has no objective but zombi control of zombis.

This is an awareness of a possible new awakening to human godhood — after most humans have been sleep-talking and sleep-walking for half a million years. The dispossessed are gambling everything on recovering their god heritage and their natural god way of life. It is something brought to focus in the words that the wildsmaidens used when taunting the dwarf who was trying to take their treasure: "If you will not forswear love as the price of a stack of chips in the zombi game, maybe you actually have something of value in you. Try to find it by joining *us* in what *we* are doing. Become a god or die."

Nietzsche stated the same idea by saying that the human race is an experiment which must fail unless man recognizes that he is only an evolutionary bridge and moves across it to become a new being.

Nietzsche chose philosophy as his medium of expression but here the need to make a choice is too immediate to be expressed in the language of philosophy. The moment of decision is tasted in the air we breathe. Wagner's strongly compelling music fits our mood. Also the story speaks to us. We see the mistakes of Wotan and Siegfried. Our advantage is that we haven't made those mistakes yet. Our problem is to think about how to succeed where the gods in the story failed — and perished.

The time cycle of opportunity for an evolutionary advance has come around again and we know our parts in the drama. To continue the direction we are now going means to become gods or die.

What I felt, and tried to define before I understood it, was everyone's prideful readiness to confirm, and repeatedly re-confirm, the decision that determines our destiny.

24.

Suddenly last night, right in the middle of a conversation, I discovered that I can now talk to Kirk in words. Up to now words have almost been a barrier between us. Last night they began to forge a new bond. The barrier of words had not been formidable. And the additional bond was not something that I was conscious of needing. But it feels wonderful to have it.

Sex, the condition of being created by the millions of years that made me a woman and Kirk a man, has up to now been the basis of our relationship. And that relationship has been solid. From the first moment in the warehouse that I walked toward him and our eyes met, my being as a woman and his being as a man has been strong enough to push aside our conflicting cultural differences. When we had our first night together the total absence of any acquired cultural mores intruding into our sexual relations emphatically confirmed this. We could easily have been the first woman and the first man in the dawn of creation, with all possible cultural worlds still waiting to be created. After we reconfirmed that experience and lived with the wonder of it for less than a week, he offered me his world without describing it, and I accepted it blindly. At that time any talk about the different cultural worlds we had known would have been impossible.

This morning we both enjoyed being silent together during breakfast. That silence confirmed that the bond between us was still solid without words. Then Kirk left. I knew he wanted to do something, somewhere, alone today while the new experience that we could talk to each other was absorbed into his whole being. I felt the same way. I wanted to be alone, think about what happened, and see how it works out to write down words to fit my new thoughts.

I have always thought of my writing as talking to Peg, or someone else from the outside world. My writing has been telling someone from the outside world about this new world and how good it makes me feel. But with the same surprising suddenness that I discovered that I can talk to Kirk, I now discover that I can no longer talk to Peg.

I sit here for awhile thinking about that.Then I realize that I cannot even talk to my old self. I have to make an effort to remember how I used to think.

I remember how puzzled I used to be trying to figure out whether Kirk was an illegal alien, whether he was a foreign spy, or just why he seemed to have trouble understanding common English words.

One time, while we were on the outside, I questioned him about some strange expression he had used and we started talking about the English language, itself. After we discussed it for some time, he came up with a comment that really floored me. He said, "The English language as you and everyone else around here uses it has no word for sex. Doesn't anyone ever think about sex and think there should be a word for it?"

I wondered what I could make of that as a clue to his background, but all I could say was, "Of course there's a word for sex; you just used it. And everybody thinks about sex more than anything else."

We were alone at one end of the company lunch room. It was a one-to-one conversation. I know that if we had been in a group, everyone would have turned off what he was trying to say by making what they thought were clever jokes. Of course, he never came up with anything like that unless we were alone. After my quick cultural group reaction, I asked him to explain what he meant. I was puzzled about everything like that he said, but that one *really* puzzled me.

"As you and everyone around here use it," he said, "the word 'sex' is a short term for 'sexual relations.' And 'sexual relations' is all that is talked about under the word 'sex.' Your dictionaries say something like 'the characteristic of being male or female.' That's a little different from sex meaning sexual relations, but the dictionaries go no further. I never hear the total picture of what sex is as a reality ever discussed. There is no word that even points to the

140

characteristic of being male or female as a reality; there's no word for sex comparable to consciousness, mass, force, inertia, will, and so on. Sex used to mean sexual relations turns the focus away from something that I think is highly important. That use of the word turns attention away from the significance of sex much more completely than was done by the puritanical taboo against mentioning it."

This is a remembered example that illustrates why I could not now talk to Peg. Here we use the same words as people outside but there are different thoughts behind the words. While outside I never did understand exactly what Kirk was saying about the word "sex." And I really tried to understand. I brought it up again two or three times and my persistence pushed him into doing some research to show me the attitude people had toward it. After his research, he told me to look up in the library a set of 50 volumes of books, edited by the editor of the Encyclopedia Britannica. The books claimed to contain the whole of Western thought. There were two volumes that claimed to be an analysis of all Western thought divided into about a hundred subjects. I looked it up and what Kirk had told me was right. Sex was not listed as one of the ideas that were set forth as the whole of Western thought. Sexual love was mentioned, but only as a subdivision of "love."

I accepted that as evidence that the world as I knew it really does not consider sex as anything even needing a word. But as long as I was in zombiland I never did see that there is an ignored reality. I never saw what people here are talking about when they use the word "sex."

"Sex" is just one example of the same word used both here and outside to express a different thought. "History," as the word is used here to refer to the past of the *human species*, has little or nothing in common with the outside world's "history" that is focused on *"nations"* and *"civilizations."* Here the words "nation" and "civilization" are not in common use. Here, those words exist only in the separate dictionaries for zombi language.

Last night, almost at the same time, Kirk and I recognized that we could now talk to each other. The week of living in intensified attention to the relationship between the people here and those outside placed me firmly at a new perspective point for viewing the whole human species. With the human species in that new perspective, the total universe also seemed to come into focus. I was no longer looking at the distorted image of reality synthesized by the zombi culture. I could see with my own eyes. And then I

141

knew, that when I could see something with my own eyes, I could use words to point to whatever I was seeing. I could discard my zombi catechism and relate my words to reality.

Last night we talked about a lot of things. As one example for me to write down and remember, I might as well continue with sex, and see if I can now use words to point out the reality that I now see.

Over and over, when touching the subject of differences between here and the outside world, everyone here has said or implied that the major point is the difference in attitude toward sex. Recalling past conversations, I recognize that this — in clear words — has been told to be by Kirk, Hans, Dag, and several others, including Inger, Lolena, and even little Bingee. But all the while, with my zombi catechism determining my thought patterns, I have lightly passed over their statements.

For awhile, trying to think for myself, I had decided that there were *two* major things that set Camp 38 at odds with the rest of the world: (1) The difference in what is an approved, socially justifiable execution, and (2) the difference in what is considered socially acceptable sexual relations and childbearing. The operas showed me that these are just two facets of one issue. Now my double image of one reality has merged because sex has come into focus.

All four nights the operas focus on sex as one reality seen from different perspectives. The theme is stated in the prelude between the wildsmaidens and the dwarf. The wildsmaidens speak for the world here; the dwarf speaks for the outside world. The conflict is between love and power. Love is sexual love, not some abstract ambiguous love that does not encompass the meaning of sex. Power is the power on which the outside world is built — the power that destroys sexual love by destroying individual integrity. It is the power that reduces people to asexual beings whose dwarf souls are the components of a manipulated group — a manipulated group in the process of becoming a group-entity.

Following the statement of the sex theme, as it is introduced in the scene between the dwarf and the wildsmaidens, the next scene is a conversation between Wotan and Fricka. They are talking about the biological evolution of sexual love.

In the outside version, Wotan mentions that he has given one of his eyes for Fricka's love. In the outside world, no one asks what that means. They don't ask because the whole is accepted as a far-fetched symbolism — some wierd, irrational pagan mythology.

A little point like giving up an eye can easily be twisted to make it fall in with "civilized" thought patterns. All simply interpret the emotional impact of so great a price as expressing Wotan's great love for Fricka. They let it go at that.

Here the actual language is not much different from the outside version. Wotan says, "Masculine combat and feminine love are two sides of one being. To become a man and know your love I surrendered half of myself." That would say nothing different to the people outside. Instead, it would detract from the drama; it would take away the dramatic imaginative picture of tearing an eye from its socket and holding it out in commercial payment.

Here the context and the background of the people in the audience combine to make Wotan's words mean he is talking about the evolutionary development of male and female from an asexual organism.

In the version here, Wotan is not a supernatural man, but his is a "god's" perspective as the word "god" is used here — that is, he is a being with a long-range view that looks at human life in relation to the total universe. That long range view is considered in every action he takes. Sex is placed in that long range perspective. Giving one eye, or surrendering half of himself refers to becoming a sexual being.

Looking at the whole of evolution, he is saying, "It is good." He is saying "yes" to life. He is saying "I approve of the evolution-ary development that produced me as a sexual being." Thinking of himself as part of the whole of life, continuing over millions of years, he is saying that he was once a self-sufficient asexual organism of cooperating cells but that he gladly gave up part of his self-sufficient being, part of his perception — and part of his capability for independent existence — in order to accept the more life-intense plateau of sex. He can say "yes" to existent reality because to accept the plateau of sex is to become *more* that a self-sufficient asexual being —even more than the outside world's concept of an omnipotent god.

Wotan's words have brought the long range view of the sex theme into focus; they have shown the significance of what is happening from the god perspective. The dwarf curses love; in his search for power, the dwarf denounces the evolutionary plateau of sex. The price of love is the price of being organically less than an asexual being; it requires abdication of asexual power. Wotan consciously accepts it because, paradoxically, what is organically less can be emotionally more — a more highly evolved emotional

143

phrase in the total melody of living.

If the story dealt in philosophical abstracts it would identify asexual organisms with the hypothesized omnipotent gods of the outside world, and identify sexual beings with the multiple gods hypothesized by the pagan Northern Europeans. But drama requires a more realistic presentation.

Because the work is dramatic, it must present reality. At first the "nations" of the outside world are presented as FAFNER and FASOLT. "Nations" are the problem; they are group entities in the process of destroying sex by becoming asexual realities. The drama presents "nations" first as giants. Although the giants are stupid they are recognizably human. The giants lose all human qualities and evolve into dragons. The dwarfs are parts (citizens) of the group-entities. The dwarfs are also the individual manipulators of those group-entities. The dwarfs are also isolated beings trying to build up a manipulated group-entity. The dwarfs are what we call zombis.

Giants and dragons are the dramatic images for nations. Dwarfs are biological humans with the dwarf souls that would denounce love in order to create powerful nations.

Wotan's words are implying (what is accepted here) that the outside world does not say "yes" to the evolutionary plateau of sex, that it will not approve the biologocal reality that exists. He is saying that, even though those in the outside world retain their sexual-sensuality, they have no real being as sexual entities. Then Wotan proclaims his refusal to surrender to the nations his being as a sexual entity — his masculinity. Fricka, the goddess of marriage, makes no comparable statement about her femininity.

This is all said in no more words than are used to say it in the outside version of the opera. The few words say fully to the people here exactly that I have said in that long drawn out statement. This is true because the people here have a cultural background that accepts all this as self-evident. Wotan needs only to *refer* to the subject; his concept of the evolutionary plateau of sex is that of the people here — something that I am just beginning to see. The people here would get the same thing from the outside version of the operas.

No one outside understands the Ring Operas as do the people here because no one outside understands the pre-theocratic viewpoint of the Northern Europeans on which the operas are built. Wagner worked from fragments left over after that viewpoint had been mutilated and lost. The mutilated fragments may say even more than Wagner *consciously* perceived. However, his artistic genius kept him faithful to the original spirit.

Here, Western, Chinese, and American Indian culture-heritages have been ground against each other. Agreements that support individual sovereignty do not require people to tolerate sophistries that others have retained from past cultural pressures. With such sophistries removed, the people seem to have reverted naturally to the same sort of innate perception of total reality that is the source of the original operas. They recognize that sex, the evolutionary flow of life that is dependent on the rhythm of separating and joining, separating and joining, continually separating and joining male and female differences, marks the forefront of all evolutionary development. They recognize that, if the overall flow of evolutionary development has a direction that can be understood intellectually, then sex is the clearest milestone from which to chart that direction. Sex is life's direction pointer.

Here, people look for the meaning of sex; they look both subjectively and objectively.

Subjectively: They recognize creative intelligence as something that exists in themselves. They do not believe that creative intelligence magically appeared with the evolutionary development of the human species. If it exists in all life, then it makes sense to talk of life's purpose and what clue sex gives to that purpose.

Objectively: They recognize that propagation cannot be the purpose of sex because asexual propagation is entirely adequate. They cannot accept sensuality as the purpose of sex when they look at the salmon beating its way up stream to spawn and see no physical contact between male and female in the sexual act.

They conclude that propagation of the species is something tied to sex so as to accent its importance, and to preserve the plateau of sex as a condition for survival. It appears that sensuality is also something tied to sex to give still further emphasis to the instinct that makes the salmon beat its way upstream to mate and die. It also appears that the *extreme* sensuality bred into the sexual act of the human species is an emphasis demanding *conscious* attention. If people are going to give conscious attention to *anything* they need to give conscious attention to the direction that sex appears to be pointing.

After honest discussions between individuals of different cultural heritages, who respect the mortal force behind each other's individual sovereignty, and who have no tolerance for verbal sophistry, it is generally accepted here that sex means life has two

145

impulses that must be continually separated and united. These are (1) creation by selective care and preservation, and (2) creation by selective destruction. Sex is a division of these two creative impulses between female and male. Both exist in every individual, but weighting the impulses on one side or the other has advantages from both the subjective and objective viewpoints.

Subjectively, a dominant impulse makes for greater emotional joy; it releases one from the tedium of making carefully reasoned philosophical choices; it encourages confident decisions and actions backed by *innate* directional approval.

Objectively, the enforced mating as a condition of continued life points up the desirability of both the two methods of creation and their necessity for complimenting each other.

That view of sex is the basis for the agreements upholding individual sovereignty here. That view of sex is the theme that runs through all the operas. That view is what makes the operas utterly incomprehensible to the outside world; here every child understands everything in them easily with no effort.

That view of sex is what requires us to have no relationship to the outside world. That view does not constitute a difference of opinion with the outside world. There is nothing that can be discussed. There is no opinion outside. Outside there is a cultural smoke screen hiding the reality that is sex. In the opera the dwarf seeking the path to power says, "I curse love." The struggle for power, on which the outside world focuses, is dependent on blocking out the reality of sex as a plateau of evolutionary development. The outside world is accurately portrayed by the dwarf who curses love.

Last night Kirk talked freely about the outside world. When he went outside he studied it as I, an anthropology major, might have studied primitive people in some back eddy untouched by "progress." To him all current "civilizations," both Western and Eastern, are no less primitive than any to which I have long applied that term. "Civilizations," in his view, are not only not making "progress" for the human species; they are pushing toward evolutionary regression. They are continuing the human regression that makes everyone, even total zombis, view primitive people who can be seen objectively, *who are not like themselves,* as beings that are lower than wild animals. Here all the outside world is seen as moving backward from evolution's advance echelon. All the outside "civilizations" are seen as opposing the evolutionary plateau of sex.

Kirk sees the attempt to distract attention from sex as one

146

continuous effort that began before known human history. It is not an open attempt that can be seen and combated. It is a smoke screen that clouds perception. The words, ideas, and cultural mores that are injected into the smoke screen vary widely but all have one purpose — obscuring perception of sex.

The injections into the smoke screen have complex ramifications. No purpose is served by examining the *ramifications*. One *example* is enough. One that has persisted for over five thousand years can be used as an example of what *all* try to do: The advocates of Hinduism hypothesize an aboriginal god of creation and then hypothesize that the god evolved into (1) a god of creation by selective preservation, and (2) a god of creation by selective destruction. This god-hypothesis serves to de-emphasize the fact that *in the world of reality* those two facets of creation belong to individual females and males — not to *abstract* gods. Those seeking to create group-entities want to ascribe both to the *group-entity* they are trying to create.

All theocracies, as well as all atheistic governments that replace theocratic "authority" with state "authority," actively add to that same old sex-obscuring smoke screen. Tolerant "democracies" are simply overwhelmed and lose all sense of direction. But always the state, church, or whatever name is given to the manipulated group on its way to become an actual entity, seeks to make the individuals that compose it into its asexual parts. The group-entity, *when it becomes real,* will simply be for its parts what the asexual organism is for its cells.

I and everyone else outside were always able to see that it is a *functional* take-over when the state or church denies an individual man's prerogative to kill on his own volition, when the state or church demands that the individual kill only as a unit of an army or police force obeying a "constituted authority." We could also see that it is a *functional* take-over when the state or church denies an individual woman's prerogative to choose her mate and bring up her children without any meddling from the hypothesized entity.

The *functional* take-over is clearly visible. It is the cultural smoke screen that destroys clear perception — and makes the functional take over possible — that I have now seen with my own eyes.

One has to see *what* is being hidden in order to see the smoke screen doing the hiding. Otherwise a world of gray smoke is accepted as the way things are. If the smoke screen is accepted, then the unperceiving zombis accept control from their manipulators.

I can see now that throughout all history the cultural smoke

147

screen put up by "civilizations" has been effective enough to limit the whole concept of sex to a source of sensual pleasure and a means of reproduction.

And, with my own eyes, I can now see the current moves in the direction of still further regression.

Current "civilizations" praise the "progress" that will have been achieved when test tube babies replace sexual reproduction. And in current "civilizations" the remaining vestige of sexual sensuality that once called attention to sex no longer does so. Undiscriminating heterosexual relations, homosexual relations, perverted practices, and group orgies are no more related to sex than the squirming of maggots in carrion.

Looking at current "civilizations" and historical "primitive societies" without distinguishing between them, Kirk equates the excessive display of pneumatic breasts and sensuous female legs in magazines, television and on giant billboards with the carving and parading of giant wooden phalli by what I have always called primitive peoples. I have known anthropology professors to suggest that comparison but I have never known them to suggest that the impulse for these displays was something of profound importance.

I, and most people I knew outside, thought all the breasts and legs on display evidenced a successful revolt against the hush-hush attitude toward sex that Judaeo-Christianity had pressured on the Western World. Kirk reminded me that "primitive people" were not revolting against Judaeo-Christianity when they focused so much attention on the phallus as a sex symbol. Also he believes that sex symbols — breasts, phalli, et cetera — are no more often symbols of fertility in ancient primitive societies than in the current one. As he and most people here view them, the public displays of these symbols in all societies are the subconscious of the people crying out for attention to the sex of which they are being deprived. In *all* cases, ancient and current, the cry is so basic, so primitively childlike, so much an endlessly repeated single word instead of a meaningful sentence, because the smoke screen is so complete that it keeps the people from consciously forming any expressible thoughts about sex. Only their subconscious impulse to think about what is being taken from them breaks through. Their attempts at conspicuous "sexiness" are nothing but a staring, pointing, idiot-like focus on some symbol of the thing for which articulate expression has been denied them.

From my first meeting with Kirk, I instinctively abandoned the "civilization" I had known for the reality of a culture-ignoring, one-to-one relationship with him. Instinctively I knew that relationship to be more than anything I had ever before glimpsed. Now I find a new wonder that I can talk to him. Now I can relate to him on a fully conscious level and be fully conscious of what he is and what I am becoming — a sexual being conscious of what one's sexual being is.

Now, remembering the outside world, I am horrified at the awareness of what I might have become if I had remained there. I might have moved along in such perfect agreement with the trend that I would never have recognized my zombi conditioning as something imposed on me. Like a million other women, I would doubtless have seized a brief moment in some swirl of faddish mass nymphomania and never have known that it was a psychotic effort to grasp the sex of which I was being deprived.

If I had remained outside until I sensed that the something I reached for had slipped through my fingers, I would have stood gazing at myself in the mirror with a pained wish not to believe what I saw. And I would never have known that it was not the loss of youth but the loss of sex which made, out of what should have been a woman, that empty-eyed, lifeless zombi that stared back at me.

25.

Today, alone here in this strangely new world, confident that Kirk will return from wherever he went today, and that the people here will want to relate to me, I find it difficult to accept as other than miraculous what has happened to me. In less than half a year, at first by blindly tying my life to Kirk's, I have committed myself to a direction diametrically opposed to that which the dominant stream of mankind has been following throughout all recorded history, and probably for a long time before.

The numerical odds against the survival of our Camp 38 may be a million to one. But that doesn't disturb me. The odds were doubtless higher for the first fish that crawled up on the land and tried to breathe air. And I have come to know that living a good life means disregarding mathematical odds and making choices dictated by the depth of my being. The discouraging odds against our success are as nothing compared to the pride that continually wells up in me for the ideal I share with the people here. As compared to the total of Homo sapiens we are an insignificant and unknown minority, unlike anything imagined by the outside world, but I feel that our dream of what we are becoming is one that can stand with honor before the tribunal of total reality.

At first my commitment was a blind grasping of a hand in the darkness, but with each increase of wakefulness I have consciously committed myself anew. Now, alone, unpressured, speaking only to myself in my greatest honesty, I want to see as clearly as possible what I am rejecting and what I am choosing.

What I am rejecting is fairly clear. I am rejecting the idea that a body-politic or group phantom is something desirable. I am also rejecting all "progress" in making such a group-phantom into a reality. Along with that rejected "progress" goes the promise of an ever-increasing array of wondrous new gadgets, and the hyperstimulation of almost instantaneous contact with four billion people all over the world and with their kaleidoscopically eye-catching activities. Also I am rejecting a generally comfortable, although sometimes repulsive, sense of oneness with all those people.

What I am choosing is more difficult to see. I suppose the same was true for the first fish that crawled up on the land. Individual freedom is only a small part of it. That is merely the outward form of the underlying significance. I am choosing a world which recognizes that the value of people each to the other comes because deep down they *are* diverse individuals, and that this diversity reaches a thundering symphonic accent as two sexes. The respect for, and encouragement of, this diversity is concretely honored by everyone's willingness to grant to everyone else his individual sovereignty if he wants it, and to grant to each individual woman an additional power to be herself because it is seen that she may better articulate her woman being by choosing not to exercise her sovereignty in the same way a man does.

Unhesitatingly I choose the way designed for a woman's special choosing. I like being a woman here as I never dreamed I could like being a woman.

Also I like being a person here, a separate living entity. The *aboriginal* oneness of all I accept as axiomatic. The outside world's frantic cry for *current* oneness with others I see as manipulated madness. Here there are no club emblems, and group-creating cliches — things that give a sense of unity by excluding everyone who is not in the same verbal swim. Here I am only I. I have no inflated sense of importance which I can hug to myself — as people do outside when they feel that they are part of a group in power, one of the leaders of a social swirl, or even simply part of the human race as distinguished from "the beasts of the field."

But here I neither need nor want any such inflated sense of importance. Here I am not afraid to be myself. By totally rejecting that illusion of importance, I can know joy in the adventure of constantly relating myself, as an individual, to the inorganic natural world, to individual plants and animals, and to other human individuals as I, a reality, am in the here and now. With no group criterion deprecating my own judgment, I can have diverse real contacts and diverse real experiences in which I, myself, have a god-like freedom, joy, and responsibility to seek out and perpetuate what *I* perceive as life's greatest values. I have a new *eagerness to be myself* because, in everyone's face, words, and actions I see joy that there is a diversity of beings, as well as joy that there are two sexes.

I see sex as an invitation extended to me by life to know intimately and to love someone *radically different* from myself. I accept it gladly. I now know Kirk is *radically* different from me — a difference I never remotely suspected could exist between a man and a woman at the time I first met him. I love the newly-discovered difference because of the greatly increased emotional tension it brings to my love of him.

Having experienced something of what it is to be a woman, I am beginning to know what it is to cast off the benumbing dream of a sleep-walker and look at reality. I feel that in getting a glimpse of the meaning of sex I am seeing as I see in the early dawn — before there is enough light to distinguish more than black and white. When my eyes are fully opened I will be able to see colors also, be able to see individual men and women in all their varieties, as they are in reality. I will no longer see them blurred by an image imposed before my eyes of what an individual-dampening culture says they should be. I only vaguely sense the unimaginable new vistas of being that will open for me in that noon-day tomorrow.

There is no need to dwell on them. Already I have a full life based on the clear perception of the black and white in today's dawn. As a woman I can give my love freely and there is no confusion as to who or what I love. Here the man I love need not be what he would be outside, a somnambulant being who vacilates between being a man and an unsexed "citizen." Nor am I asked to love a fictitious entity called a "sovereign state." Here *my* sovereign and the one to whom I offer my love is one fully-integrated, flesh and blood man — different from me, but a real being that can be seen and touched, a being whose children I can bear.

Unlike the vestigial men outside, the man I love, like the others here, chooses to live under conditions where he stands in full view and insists on being accepted or rejected by all others as a *whole being*. He refuses to take a hand in manipulating mobs of status seekers who have been reduced to nothing but idiot-like game players. He refuses to play a dark game where he hides a puny "private life" behind a ridiculous "public image." He lives as a *whole* man or dies as a *whole* man. He has agreed to meet others of his kind with the clear understanding: "I am what I am — an undivided whole. I will not be factored. Let anyone who wants to oppose my *whole* being declare himself my enemy and draw his sword."

I am a woman and I could never feel that constant mortal defiance. But I can love a man whose integrity is strong enough to make him feel like that. This is a wholly new kind of love. My loving and my pride in the act of choosing who to love have become a single emotion.

No dream world that my wildest hopes might once have created could possibly approach the grandeur of the here and now.

26.

We are all millionaires! We are worth hundreds of millions of dollars! Hundreds and hundreds of millions! Billions! We have an enormous private yacht. We own enormous amounts of land and lots of factories scattered across three continents and several islands. The Camp 38 Company is a holding company and all the people here are the stockholders. I am not but Kirk is. And my children born here will automatically become stock holders. The wealth is so great that if it were divided up every man, woman and child would still probably be a millionaire — maybe many times a millionaire. I can't get used to the idea. It staggers me.

I had suspected that Gilbert had left this land to the people here after it had been logged off, and maybe set up a continuing trust fund to keep the taxes paid, but I wasn't prepared for this. It means nothing to anyone here but Kirk knew it would be a dramatic discovery to me and, as usual, he let me have the fun of making that discovery myself.

Camp 38 includes a stretch of ocean beach and we just came from there. Kirk knew he would have to tell me everything when we went to the ocean so he has been putting off taking me until he thought I was ready for it. I think I was ready. But ready or not I've now been exposed to the full facts about Camp 38.

The chariot roads don't go through all the way to the beach so we started out on horseback. On the way, the horse trail goes along a creek and through an underpass where a highway crosses it high above. The woods are thick and the highway is screened with trees so we couldn't see it but I could hear cars passing by. This was what Kirk had been keeping from me by putting off our ocean trip. I'm glad he didn't tell me beforehand. Finding it was a big experience.

When we came to the place and I heard the sounds above I knew at once they were cars and trucks. I reined up and looked around. I looked at him in wonder. He understood of course how I felt but he didn't say anything. With electrical excitement running up and down my spine I dismounted. I felt like an explorer who has come upon some long lost civilization — silent and awed before the totally unbelievable. Kirk dismounted, too, and took the reins of my horse from me, saying casually, "I'll give the horses a drink." While he led the horses down to the creek I edged up toward the level of the highway. The ground was clear under the trees. There were easy trails climbing up the rocks; so it was clear that I wasn't the first to be interested in the noise from the highway. But before I got where I could see anything I came to a high stone fence topped by a cyclone fence and barbed wire. It would have taken a lot of ingenuity and work to get over it. I supposed it could be done, of course, but I didn't try it. I went back and met Kirk with a smile of defeat. He gave me an understanding smile but didn't say anything when we remounted.

The trail was wide enough to ride side by side at this stretch and he set a walking pace alongside me and explained. "I know you are wondering how this sort of thing can be. That highway crossing Camp 38 is a nuisance but to keep access to the ocean we have to put up with it. It's really less trouble than you'd think. It's explained simply and honestly to children here and has never been a problem from this side. Across the canyon there is another fence like the one you saw. We own the land all around on the other side of both fences and we've located chemical processing plants in a way that gives us an understandable excuse for guarding the area. The chemical factories are all operated by zombis and the guards are zombis but it has never caused us any trouble. It's a simple matter of arousing no one's curiosity."

Then I learned for sure what I had gradually come to suspect;

the whole secret of how Camp 38 can exist is a simple matter of arousing no one's curiosity. But the problem is much different with enormous wealth than it was as I had imagined it. In some ways it's easier. In some ways it's harder. But the possibilities of what we can do if we run into trouble are so many that it gives me a much safer feeling. If the nations that claim jurisdiction over our lives and the land we live on become too meddlesome in the way we live, we can move to islands or other continents where others claim jurisdiction until the trouble has blown over.

I found all this out several days ago and I'm still staggered by it. I understood quickly something I already knew but had been puzzled about. The issuing of great quantities of scrip is the formal payment of dividends, and the burning of last year's issue is putting practically all the earnings back into the corporation. But the apparent ease with which we maintain undisturbing contact with the outside world is almost unbelievable.

I was just beginning to recover from the meaning of those unseen cars passing overhead and the factories operated by zombis and owned by us when I got the second shock. We had ridden less than an hour more when I caught the smell of the ocean and learned that the "creek" we had been riding beside was really a small river and that in a few kilometers it would empty directly into the ocean. It widened and deepened some and a little further on we came to a dock alongside it and a seagoing ship!

After learning that we owned zombi operated factories I was ready to suspect that the ship was a zombi operation. However I could hardly believe we were running a ship-line and I asked Kirk about it. He said we had steamship lines operated by zombis but this was our yacht. It is much bigger than any yacht I had ever seen. It is simply a small ocean going liner. But it is operated by people who actually live here with no thought of commercial use.

We went aboard and I found that I knew both of the two men who were taking care of it that day; I had danced with them at my acceptance party. Kirk.had rotated at the job they were doing in times past and knew his way around thoroughly. He showed me around and we only talked to the men a little. Everything was very luxurious aboard. It was so much out of keeping with the way people here live that I asked about it. Keeping down curiosity was the explanation Kirk gave me. The ship sails into zombi ports and people would talk about a private yacht that wasn't luxurious; also the evidence of luxury awes most zombis and causes them to keep their distance.

The ocean was only a few kilometers further. There are several kilometers of beach with twenty or thirty cabins. Any that are vacant can be taken and used. Everyone here, of course, leaves the cabins in welcoming cleanness. We had a choice of several and stayed in one that I will always love. It was very old and built of logs but as nice inside as our home. There was a little fireplace with a cooking pot and grill swinging over it and a big window seat that looked out on the ocean.

I was surprised to find the pantry stocked with food brought in from the outside, cans and jars with commercial labels on them. The trail has deliberately been made so narrow that no one can bring chariots all the way down. There is always a chance of someone coming here from the ocean and chariots would arouse interest, as would food in anything but ordinary containers. So everything is brought in by ship and looks very ordinary. Although the cabins are tastefully furnished, the furniture is more ordinary than that usually seen here. Some of it even carries standard brand names.

We stayed four nights at the beach. Then we stayed two days and nights aboard the ship as our tour of duty for the year. The idea ia to keep two people aboard at all times when it's not in use. Those caring for it also are prepared to meet any zombis who might chance to get into the beach area. Everyone who goes to the ocean or does duty on the yacht is made fully acquainted with how to escort any zombis, who might possibly get in, back to the outside without arousing suspicion. It has been several years now since the last time it happened; two boys washed ashore in a small boat that capsized.

Apparently with adequate wealth and careful consideration the handling of these matters isn't very difficult. To the outside world this is just private timber land used in part as residences by the owners and their presumed employees. Every child here grows up knowing that we are a little handfull of people in a big world that would not tolerate our non-conformity if it knew, and that we are not big enough to fight it. They all learn that we have to keep contacts to the minimum possible to avoid having outsiders turn on us like a hive of bees and try to make us into zombis.

Simple!

Really it's not even unusual. After all it's the way every intelligent person in zombiland lives in his own home and with his own little circle of friends. Everyone even makes and lives by his own laws or private code of morals which his friends understand and share. Usually their own worlds are just a state of mind, or a few hours out of each day, or an occasional short vacation away from it all that sometimes magically seems something real. Ours is nothing but a more complete separation and a more formal and positive commitment to ourselves and to others.

27.

I remember that when I was studying what little is known of the people of Northern Europe before they were overrun by theocracy, I was impressed by what the early historian, Tacitus, had to say about the use of a number to designate honor. Among the warrior peoples each tribe had what they called simply the "Hundred." It was a band of a hundred of the best men who stayed armed and ready to meet an invading enemy — men who would fight to the death against any odds and so buy time to give the others a chance to prepare for battle. The danger was great but the tradition of steadfast dependability and heroism was such that there was no greater honor than being drawn into the select band and becoming one of the Hundred. The meaning of the word and the concept behind it was perverted by the Catholic Church and the Hundred became a unit of political organization when the Church theocracy controlled Northern Europe.

The original pagan idea was fully carried over when, in Camp 38 about sixty years ago, there was organized the Hundred. The honor of belonging is in the old tradition. There's a card file (open for all to see) of possible future replacements. Each member has ten votes for replacements and a first vote cast for anyone is a nomination that puts his card on file. When any person has ten votes the nominee is placed in line as a replacement. The votes themselves are significant honors, often pointing up exemplary conduct. The votes can also be withdrawn to publicly point up disapproval of conduct. The number of members is rigidly kept and it is also rigidly kept to fifty men and fifty women.

At first I was surprised that women were included. That was before I learned what constitutes training and the expected battle lines. The training is nothing but a studied acquaintance with the zombi way of life. The possible battle is helping to manage and use our multimillion dollar empire in zombiland in a way to protect our interest rather than conform to zombi purposes.

The "armory" (known here as the zombi museum) consists of a large dwelling house, constructed and furnished in what I would

156

call upper middle class luxury, and an office with a large luxurious executive suite and conference room. No detail is missing. Telephones and intercoms connect all parts of the house and offices. There are several television sets each showing a taped recording of a typical full days television program. These are kept up-to-date with current types of programs and commercials. Radios also have typical taped programs. The idea of taped rather than live programs appears to be that of avoiding any real interest in zombi events. Newspapers and magazines are strewn about; they are current enough to be typical but old enough so that what is presented as big, exciting news has already been shown to be zombi routine. Movies and slides, showing all phases of zombi life in several countries, are also part of the training material.

From time to time members of the Hundred give anyone who wants it a conducted tour of the museum including several day's acquaintance with television, radio, slides, and movies.

I probably shouldn't say anyone who wants it. There are those who are persuaded to visit, and there are those who insist on doing so when no one who is fully acquainted with them thinks their interest is timely and purposeful. Children are seldom shown through and every attempt is made to avoid letting the museum become idle entertainment. As in everything else here the tension between personalities is the everyday working pressure that keeps the overall direction.

An attempt is made to give an education in zombi life to everyone who is going outside, whether one of the Hundred or not. Almost everyone in the Hundred is at least thirty-five years old and those who get an urge to go outside as an adventure rather than a duty are usually younger. Kirk became acquainted with the outside first through the museum when he let it be known that he was going out. He and I went through after we returned from the ocean. This was furthering my education on the relationship between us and zombiland.

When I first learned how many factories and such things we own I thought there would need to be extensive relations between us and the outside. Actually there is very little more than I originally suspected. We make much use of trust companies to manage our holdings and almost never interfere in the actual management. If we don't like the way management of a company is going we simply "sell" it to another that we own that is being run in a way we like. The directors of Camp 38 Company have full knowledge of how to play the zombi game with the phantoms called corporations. The

157

operation affects the people here no more than if the directors got together occasionally for a game of monopoly. We prefer to invest in basic industries, preferably those like lumber and food growing which involve great amounts of land. In addition to the fact that practically all dividends have been plowed back into capital for over sixty years, a great part of our increase in wealth has come from owning great quantities of cheaply bought land that later became valuable. Because of this and because we need remote land for setting up other places like Camp 38 the amount of land involved is a big consideration in all transactions.

In long range planning we are fully aware that wealth based upon some government's defending our peaceful possession of it is worthless. Mass manipulators seem to take over all governments. Nothing has real value in our eyes but people. The ultimate purpose of everything done is keeping mobs of zombis from meddling in our lives. Because we have great wealth everyone on the outside accepts the bare statement that children here are privately educated. Because we pay taxes on such a big scale the "company houses" in Camp 38 are not individually inspected. Liberal appraisals are accepted by our agents "as a concession for not disturbing the eccentric owners who choose to live quiet, retiring lives." Training in that sort of language and when to use it is training for the Hundred in "armament" and "strategy."

All the people sent out to represent us are agents of the company with very limited powers for the time they are out. Legally everyone ceases to be an owner or officer when he leaves here. Seven directors, who choose their successors, have final authority to make all decisions until that authority is revoked by the stockholders here. This has not been done for the whole eighty years. If they go outside they cease to be directors while out. A condition of being a stockholder is to be born here and to have lived nine of the last ten years here, including the last year. Kirk will not become a stockholder again until a full year since his return. The idea is that directors and stockholders must always be answerable individually to every other individual under the personal agreements here; no one who is not answerable has any authority in company matters or any wealth.

However anyone going out is ordinarily provided plenty of money by a quick vote of the directors. No one would wish to save himself by hurting his family or friends here and all realize that when they go out they will be abandoned, if necessary, to avoid bringing attention to our operation. That is, we would not risk a big court trial to defend anyone.

The directors usually come from the Hundred but are separate from it. As part of their training a portion of the Hundred usually attend director's meetings, which for educational purposes are carried on in typical zombi fashion. All of the Hundred take jobs for brief periods in as many of our companies as they can get around to in the tenth of their time they spend outside. This is acquainting themselves primarily with the way of life in the outside world. Only to a very lesser extent is it observing the operations of our companies with a view to changing their management. When they are outside our people are very seldom identified as being known by the owners and almost never pushed into decision-making positions. The Hundred are merely trained and ready to move quickly if there should be a need for it.

When I first learned the name of the group and learned that the name was really intended to associate it with the heroic Hundred of the warrior peoples, I thought it was ludicrous. I thought it must be some sort of dead-pan humor that was escaping me. To hold the positions held by the directors and the Hundred would not be considered a sacrifice in the outside world. It would be the highest goal of most people's lifetime of work. But as I watched Kirk's attitude and the attitude of those showing us through the museum, the physicist's idea of positive and negative matter that I had thought of when I went through the trading post came back to me. What is a high goal to the zombis is here a distasteful job to be done. When I fully appreciated the attitude of the people here I recognized that the use of the Hundred name was justified. In preserving the way of life of the protected people as much depends on the fidelity, courage, training, and intelligence of the Hundred here as it did in the warrior prototype. And the extent of the self-sacrifice and heroism is no less great. This realization came to me only after I had time to think about it and to consider my intimate knowledge of Kirk's experience outside as a concrete example.

All my life I have been awed when I thought about the dangers and the loneliness of a spy behind enemy lines. I have wondered what sort of people could accept lives that were such complete lies. Here individual integrity and honesty in every relation with the people around is probably more important than it is to any other people in the world. And perception of individuals and sensitivity to another's mood is much more intense among people here than anywhere else. For those who grow up under these conditions to go out and live under a false identity and watch people around

159

them enmeshed in their self-destroying zombiism — to come to like or love them, and be unable to be honest with them — must certainly be no less an emotional hurt than dying in battle with understanding comrades at one's side. Those who are chosen for it and who accept its full responsibility deserve the honor associated with being "One of the Hundred."

28.

At the entrance to the big, luxurious room where the Camp 38 directors hold their meetings a sign with the words "Conference Room" hangs over the door. Underneath in smaller letters is the name "The Primitive Room." An outsider would think this name was given to the room because of the big painting that hangs on the wall at the head of the conference table. From my knowing Kirk, who calls what I call the "civilized people," the "primitive people," I could see that "Conference Room" and "Primitive Room" are really just synonymous terms in the language of the people here. It is a room where the directors of Camp 38 relate to the outside world.

The picture that dominates the room immediately suggest a jungle village and a ceremony of some sort among a tribe of savages. There are grass huts in the background and the foreground is dominated by several weird looking figures in hugh wooden masks. The masks are all different and I suspect that each may have a significance but the total effect was all I got when I saw the picture. The men wearing the masks are grouped around a heavy table of the sort that might have been brought ashore from a ship grounded on the rocks. There is about their postures, and the light falling on the group, a solemnity suggesting that they are engaged in offering some sacrifice. But on looking closer one sees that they are playing a game on the table. One is throwing an ivory die and four odd shaped pieces of bone. Grouped in front of the players, apparently as the objects played for, are articles of jewelry, voodoo charms, a crucifix, a seal, several coins, a photograph, and numerous articles that I didn't take time to look at carefully.

Nothing identifies the race of skin color of the masked figures. The faces are all hidden by the huge masks, the bodies are covered with hairy skins or scaly hides of snakes or crocodiles, and on their hands they all wear soiled white dress gloves.

Off in the background, but so arranged in the composition

160

that the eye is drawn to them, there are some children playing with a dog and a sailboat in a puddle. They are of various races. Some are conspicuously white and blond. That brings to mind the question of what they are doing in a setting one associates with dark-skinned savages. Again one is made to think of a ship run aground. The possible fate of their parents at the hands of the masked figures, who could be playing with the remains of the parent's possessions, is brought to mind. The sacrificial attitude of the figures around the table brings out the horror on which routine stories of civilized people falling among savages usually dwell.

Then studying the goulish figures, looking for the sort of people behind the masks, I found suggestions that *some* of those behind the masks could be the parents of the out-of-place children. Apparently they would have entered the primitive game in a gamble to save themselves and their children. But I found something in the enthusiastic position of some of the hands that suggested a new horror — suggested that the once reluctant players were in danger of getting carried away with the game and going native.

The picture is unsigned; no one knows who painted it. It has a little brass plaque on it that reads: "Presented to Camp 38 Company, Inc. by Gilbert Durrell. Autumn 43, Year 55."

Gilbert was not a painter. Whether he commissioned the picture or simply saw it somewhere and recognized, with almost clairvoyant insight, what it could say to the people here almost a century later no one knows. But everyone sees its significance, and interprets the wording on the plaque as a silent request for constant re-examination of our relationship to the outside world.

I wish I could have known Gilbert Durrell.

29.

The assembly house files contain a full record of all combats. I searched through them and read everything available on the three people Kirk's father killed of the four he brought in. I think I have the full story. It's something that my children will be interested in and something Peg would want to know if I offered to bring her here. So I want to put all the pieces together and see how it sounds in organized, factual form.

Kirk's father, Karl, came from a typical midwestern town in Oklahoma. There he went to public school, occasionally went to church, and worked summers on farms or in small garages and grocery stores. The combined emptiness of a rural life trying to take pride in an earthiness it no longer possessed, and a small town trying to ape an urbanity its people couldn't conceive, made him feel the whole world was a sham.

Karl managed an escape of sorts by developing an interest in the history of other places and other times. By reason of his own heritage, and by reason of his rejection of anything resembling the world he knew, he quickly focused on Northern Europe and the life there before Roman Catholic theocracy. He devoured everything on the subject written by Julius Caesar and Tactitus. He then used their recorded facts as a catalyst to separate the original ideas in Norse and German mythology, in the Icelandic Eddas, in the story of Ossian and the Fianna in Ireland, and in everything else of the nature from the mutilating modifications inserted by theorcratic monks. What he found recreated in his mind the sort of world that was his heritage and the sort of world in which he wanted to live.

Apparently Karl was physically very vigorous. Anyway he was not satisfied to spend his life in an unreal world. He wanted to get to the world he knew had once existed. He began to study Hindu mysticism for the purpose of discovering if one could actually move through time and space. He wanted to transfer himself to the world that he found more compatible with his being.

Trying to make his conception of his chosen world more real, he began painting detailed pictures of the Northern Europeans and their activities in the era when their segregation from the rest of the world was virtually absolute. He developed impressive ability as a painter.

At nineteen he went to Kansas City and got a job in an "art studio" — designing labels for food packages. He had been there less than six months when his beginning career as a commercial artist was replaced by military service.

One of the first places he touched after getting out of the Midwest was San Francisco. It made such a strong impression on him that he later took his military discharge there. When discharged he was twenty-three. He had quite a bit of service pay, no ties, and no positive ambitions, but he had seen enough varied worlds in the realm of reality to recognize that he had the prerogative and obligation to make his own. He rented a small apartment in an old house on Green Street and began to feel the rekindling of a nascent love affair that had flamed briefly when he was passing through before. The love affair was not with a girl but with the city and geography of San Francisco.

He loved San Francisco as many other sensitive people have done, particularly poets and painters — in a way that I probably can't fully understand because I was born there and never really detached it from myself. For several months, perhaps more than a year, he lived alone and painted the hodge-podge street scenes, hills, bay, waterfront, boats — all the things that other artists paint. Some of his work sold and he began evolving into what everyone thinks of a typical artist; he even developed one of the standard eccentricities that endear artists to art worshippers. He revived and pursued his old interest in the mysticism of Oriental religions.

However this interest went too far and upset the "type" he was becoming. Taking mysticism too seriously for it to be just an interesting eccentricity, he decided to go into a prolonged hermitage to meditate and find himself. Instead of doing this in a dingy garret so as to draw attention to himself as a colorful personality, he took a map of the world and looked for areas of sparce population where he thought he could live by hunting and fishing.

Having chosen a big blank spot on the map, he got as close as possible by commercial transportation, hiked into the area, built a cabin, and began his hermitage. Then something happened to him. Really it was two things: He found Jan who became Kirk's mother, and he found Camp 38.

Although he later denounced all institutional religions, including those of the Orient, he never quite got over the feeling that his choice of the place for his hermitage and what happened might have been directed by some intuitive insight — something bordering on the occult. I often felt that way when I first came here, so it's easy for me to understand how he felt.

I can identify with Karl easily in so far as his first impression of Camp 38 is concerned. He had been living alone for nine or ten months and, except during two times when he had hiked out for tools and supplies, he had seen no human being. He was fully convinced that the big area he had chosen, showing no roads or towns on the map, was totally uninhabited. In late winter, when there was several feet of snow, and the many animals he had come to know as his only companions were holed up, the sense of isolation was still more.

Then, on such a day, when he was out on skis, feeling that he was a lone man in one-to-one communion with a universe devoid of all other human life, he suddenly caught sight of Jan. He saw her across a valley. She also was on skis and had gone further afield than usual with the same feeling he had of being alone in a universe of blue sky and snow covered hills. They saw each other about the same time. Both stared in unbelief, then both started toward the other. Flushed and breathless they met in the level of the valley that had been between them.

Jan was greatly surprised and excited; she had been born in Camp 38 and had never before come upon anyone from the outside world. But Karl was much more excited. He believed that something supernatural was surely happening.

Since my coming here was a slightly similar experience, I can understand that everything from then on added to his feeling that somehow he, or the universe, had slipped into another dimension of reality. It began with Jan's explanation of who she was and where she came from. That was like something out of his most fantastic dreams. Although obviously delighted at seeing him she didn't "relate" to any place he mentioned. He was convinced that she could not belong to the mundane world he knew. She was an intensely heightened, flesh and blood ideal of the early German women that Caesar and Tacitus had said were treated as if they were goddesses. He was ready to believe that he had actually gone back in time and space to prehistory Northern Europe as he had visualized it.

Apparently Jan and Karl were as if made for each other, and both felt it from the first. Karl's impression that he was involved in a non-understandable time-slip doubtless accented his emotional response to the contact between their different worlds. However he didn't mention it to Jan. He didn't want to alienate himself from her by talking about things to which she didn't relate. The wonder and joy to be found in exploring their differences was something they both approached with a sensitivity that did not squander its value.

Jan had been planning to spend the night alone in one of our little outpost cabins. She took him with her to it. It was almost dark when they got there. They built a fire, shared the food both were carrying, and spent most of the night sitting huddled together before the fire finding out their incredible differences and samenesses. Toward morning they fell asleep, each awakening in turn, tending the fire and making the other comfortable, until late in the morning.

That day they came the rest of the way here.

Karl was told about and shown the agreements here. At first, they appeared to him as proof positive that he had found the Northern European culture before theocracy. The agreements were exactly the ones that his studies of history had shown to be fully accepted by his ancestors twenty-five hundred years ago. However, he had always thought of them as being fully accepted without being formally put into words. He was surprised to find that, not only were they written but, they were written in English — not in ancient Northern European runes. His occult explanation was gradually giving way to an assumption that Camp 38 resulted from a pocket of pre-theocratic culture that had somehow remained unaltered over the centuries. Current English instead of ancient German was the only piece that did not fit his assumption.

But that seemed of little importance. He readily signed the agreements and accepted the conditions of life here without reservations. Then, until after Jan's death, he never left, except to take her back and show her the cabin he had built and in which he had lived alone in the woods.

Kirk was their only child, but they had five years together that seem to have been the happiest possible. When Kirk was not quite four years old, Jan was killed in a landslide.

Karl plunged into a deep depression for several months. When he began to function again, he went back to his earlier practice of probing into religions, into philosophy, and into science and history. Apparently deprived of the real woman he had loved, he reverted to thinking about people as masses and the "culture worlds" they create. He weighed the numerical odds against the survival of the Camp 38 way of life and decided to take another look at the outside world.

Going back to San Francisco, he rented an apartment like the one he had before. There he began a new hermitage in a world of people he now looked upon as everyone here looks upon the people in the outside — as an evolutionary species in a dead-end direction. He wanted to do something to jar the zombis into wakefulness.

It was this impulse, and another seemingly occult gathering together of circumstances, that caused him to take a step that was destined for tragedy.

He was spending practically all his time in the University of California Library at Berkeley, studying the history and myths of all peoples, when he got interested in a group of pseudo-intellectuals — the sort that is always starting an off-beat movement on a college campus. These were the "Individualists of the World." They had grown out of a "Citizens of the World" movement that wanted a one-world government and denounced citizenship in nations in favor of citizenship in the world. The Individualists not only denounced citizenship in a nation but the whole concept of citizenship. They were going to do away with war over the face of the earth and their slogan was "Only citizens fight wars."

Their rallies were well-attended and the speakers who denounced the concept of nations and the concept of citizenship were enthusiastically applauded. It sounded to Karl as if their objective was a world-wide Camp 38. He sought out the leaders and got to know them. His idea was to study their plans and decide if he thought the movement could be made to work on a world-wide scale.

Karl looked like a real find to them. He was tall and well-built like Kirk, older than any of them, had military combat experience, and a fund of historical and philosophic knowledge. They thought he could be an asset to their movement and cultivated him.

For Karl's part he was highly impressed with the ability and dedication of the four; there were two boys and two girls.

The oldest, Ward, was twenty-three and was of an appearance and personality that gave the movement a sense of dignity and stability. He was basically an organizer and leader.

Margaret, then eighteen, was very pretty and as Ward's girl friend enhanced his appearance.

The real drive was furnished by Giles, a man of less impressive appearance than Ward, and only twenty, but a fiery orator whose own voice had such a hypnotic effect on him that when he began talking to a group he virtually went into a mystic trance and put together the words and ideas that would appeal to them as if he were in telepathic communion with the whole group consciousness.

The fourth member, Edith, was a behind-the-scenes inciter for Giles. She was twenty-two, rather homely and bookish looking but wise enough not to make her pitches on the speaker's platform. She was a strategy planning oracle who made a cult of Oriental religions and strongly implied that she possessed extraordinary insights. She constantly fed Giles ideas and, by a highly practical nature that hid its machinations behind a preoccupied trance-like exterior, she isolated and welded the four into an exclusive high command for the movement. Her apartment, which she provided with a good supply of food and drinks, was the headquarters for strategic planning.

Edith strongly resented the intrusion of Karl when he was first brought to her apartment. But his obviously sincere interest in her mystical claims, together with the fact that his detached bystander attitude seemed to pose no threat to her power, caused her to welcome him fully after the first meeting.

After it is all over and I look back knowing what happened, it seems to me that Karl must have been less perceptive than he might be expected to be. But maybe not. I, myself, can make arguments against my opinion. Although he was over five years older than the oldest in the group, his background had given him no opportunity to study the motivations of revolutionists. These free-thinking intellectualists revolting against the faults he recognized in the decaying culture into which he had been born seemed to him the possible salvation of the world. I can *almost* understand that. Anyway, he began drawing on his knowledge of Camp 38 to give practical shape and strength to their objectives.

Apparently they climbed over the ideas he set before them like vines over a trellis. Before long he became convinced that all they needed to assure the success of their movement was a concrete concept that would save all the energy they wasted on vacillating directions; he wished that he could introduce them to the life here.

Then, just at the moment when the empathy between Karl and the group had reached its peak, and would have collapsed if not shored up, the means for shoring it up seemed to appear with occult timeliness. On his way home from an all night discussion of ideology in Edith's apartment — the most serious talk the five had ever had jointly — he saw our yacht tied up at a dock in San Francisco. Its appearance just at that moment seemed miraculous to him. An idea and plan flashed into his mind full-formed except for one point. He went into a waterfront restaurant and had breakfast while he pondered over ways of overcoming the obstacle.

He wanted to take the four to Camp 38 for a visit and back again so they could have the benefit of standing up their nebulous ideas against a concrete reality. But he knew he could not let them know where they had been.

He remembered his own feeling on being suddenly confronted with Camp 38, the feeling that he had passed into another dimension of existence. He believed that the impression could be sustained for several weeks by a studied effort. He also thought the four were fully enough steeped in hazy occult possibilities to accept an irrational explanation of the experience that would be believed by no one if they later tried to tell it as actual fact. The only trouble was that he couldn't believe that whoever was then in charge of the ship would let him bring them.

He knew that he would have no trouble going aboard and returning to Camp 38 himself, but he could expect some opposition to bringing even one outsider with him, and he believed four would be so strongly opposed that he would have no chance. Perhaps because he did not grow up here, he yielded to what everyone here recognizes as the most persuasive and most dangerous temptation. He put the great numbers to be benefited into the scales against the danger to a few; he let nothing but the weight of numbers persuade him to a rash plan of shadowy honesty.

He made a decision while he was having breakfast, then went aboard and found Dag acting as captain for the voyage. Anyone else he might have found in charge would, he thought, have given his plan a better chance. But he decided to try to push it through anyway. He found that the ship was sailing direct for Camp 38 that night and asked if he could come along. Assured that he could, he asked, acting as if it were an afterthought about something that didn't really matter much, if he could bring some stuff with him perhaps half a ton or less. Finding he could, he asked the exact time of sailing and said he would try to make it with his stuff by that time and if he didn't to go on without him.

Then he did the thing that, despite all else he later did, made Dag so untrusting of him that he has only recently, since I have been here, begun to get over his suspicions of Karl's son.

Karl made some preparations that day. Then that night he invited the four over to his apartment. He offered them an "out of the world" experience if they would sign the agreements we live by.

Wondering whether he was mad, or if there really was something to the occult ideas they all professed to believe and thought he was saying could be proved, they decided to go all out and accept his offer to show them the world for which they were striving. They signed the agreements. Also he had them write notes to their friends saying they were going into a joint seclusion and meditation for several months.

Then, without their knowing it, he drugged their drinks. As soon as they were unconscious, he packed them in four excelsior padded crates with air holes that he had prepared that day. He then trucked the boxes to the waterfront and got them hoisted aboard and lashed down on deck just in time for the ship to sail.

When they were well out on the high seas he told Dag what he had done. Dag had the crates opened and found four unconscious people packed in excelsior.

For a few minutes the half unpacked people still lay on the deck in the boxes while Karl tried to explain. The explanation brought up so many questions that, after awhile, he and Dag put the unconscious four on comfortable bunks below and Karl continued the explanations in the saloon.

Still undecided as to whether to turn back and risk the publicity or seek some other solution, Dag invited everyone aboard into the saloon to hear Karl's ideas. Everyone understood that turning back or going on was Dag's decision. But the danger was to everyone at Camp 38 and the one endangering them was in their midst. So Dag wanted it known by as many as possible as soon as possible.

It speaks well for Karl's behavior during the five years he had already been at the camp that he was able to talk to all the people aboard and they all heard him out without unequivocal condemnation. After being questioned half the night by a roomful of vitally concerned people, and so being made to think of many facets of his act that hadn't occured to him before, Karl felt much less sure of his plan. He doubted that he could, without creating trouble, return any of the four to the outside world after they had been here. He changed his plan: He decided that he wanted to try to bring them into a permanent part of the life here. He told everyone that he, himself, would personally see that they did not cause trouble.

A significant point in causing other to believe that bringing them on might be the best course was the fact that Karl showed the four signed agreements.

Dag never elaborated on the basis for his decision but he didn't turn back and try to get the unwelcome passengers ashore before they were allowed to wake up.

The sea became rough that night and when they did wake up late next day they all became violently seasick. They hardly left their cabins all day and their physical sensations occupied their thoughts more than the question of where they were and what had happened to them.

The seasickness may have had an effect. Maybe the occult leanings were all sham from the beginning. Anyway they never had any inclination to put a transcendental interpretation on the experience. All four suddenly forgot their intellectual ideals and began to play the zombi world's standard game. The leader of the transformation was the same Edith who had led them to accept mysticism. Overnight the translike stare in her eyes gave way to the appraising coldness of a banker looking for an angle to make some personal gain.

Our yacht spoke clearly of wealth. The source and control of that wealth at once became of paramount interest to three of the four Individualists.

Before they were here a week Margaret ceased to be one of the "Individualists" and became an individual. She made friends quickly and was fully accepted everywhere. The other three became a closer knit clique.

Their constant questions about the contrast between the simple way of life here and the wealth implied by the yacht soon became irritating to everyone they met. Their persistent probing alienated them. But mostly they held together and made their plans together just because they chose to do so.

Karl tried to get them to stay away from each other completely for awhile. He even arranged individual invitations for them into separate groups. But the three from outside insisted on sticking together so closely that they came to be known as "the conspirators."

"Conspirators" or "revolutionists" seemed a much more appropriate name for them than "Individualists." Their behavior pattern seemed to be conditioned to such an extent that they were not individually motivated persons. They had suddenly found themselves in a world in which the objectives they claimed to be seeking were fully accomplished. Instead of doing what Karl had thought they would, instead of trying to make a more careful measurement of their ideals by standing them alongside the accomplished reality, they began looking for ways to use the talents they had displayed in arousing violent dissent against "the establishment" on the college campus. They *talked* of carrying the individualism of Camp 38 to the rest of the world. But in everything they *did* it was clear that they were trying to bring the outside world's typical revolutionary group tactics to Camp 38. To them Camp 38 was a bunch of screwballs who were ripe for exploitation.

Most young people here, who plan to have children together and start a family life, also like to build their houses themselves; so there are quite a number of vacant houses. These are dedicated by plaques on them to the use of lovers, wayfaring strangers, and such wordings. Shelter was no problem for the three, and at first food was not.

They arrived just before the spring planting; there is always an abundance of food; and following what was known as an unoffensive zombi custom, everyone wanted to bring them some token of welcome. They were loaded down with choice offerings of food.

They ate the food given them but they showed little enthusiasm for participating in the work of any of the groups who invited them. The invitations were soon withdrawn. Karl helped them get started on a field of their own but they only worked in desultory fashion. Food became a problem. The main staple of their diet was deer Karl shot and gave them. They even let a fresh cow he gave them for milk go dry from lack of attention. They never asked to be taken back to the outside world but they obviously didn't want the way of life compatible with the concepts here.

They went through the whole spring before things came to a climax. It took them that long to get their teeth into the facts they had been probing for. They didn't really learn the vast extent of our wealth but they learned that Camp 38 is a holding company whose holdings include a timber company which they knew by name to be a very big one. Also they learned that everyone here is an equal stockholder and that the seven directors control only because that authority has been delegated to them "until revoked."

They recognized that legally all decisions could be made by a manipulated majority just as they are outside. This was a field for their talents. They seized it with a return of the full enthusiasm engendered by the memory of their past successes on the campus.

People here didn't respond to mass rallies. But since there are less than five thousand people here, they saw this as a fertile field for person to person proselytizing. Swaying stockholders votes was a positive goal of success that could be measured mathematically.

The first goal of these revolutionists was limited with veteran cunning. They only asked stockholders to revoke authority delegated to the directors and have monthly meetings. Their new revolutionary line equated democratic voting processes and individual freedom. All the cliches of this line were new and fresh to the people here and it began to look as if a joyfully enthusiastic and intensive presentation of sophistries might be successful. Karl recognized that it might. Those sophistries had been honed by mass manipulators for countless centuries, and Karl had spent much time studying their efficacious history.

Of course the conspirators concentrated on the young. Soon a nucleus of those interested began to gather for discussions. Disciples of the new faith began to bring food and the three abandoned all pretense of working; they devoted their full time to bringing enlightenment on the advantages of the outside world. These advantages, which they had ridiculed when they were outside, they now upheld as wonderful things of which the youth of Camp 38 were being deprived.

Karl demanded that they stop all these activities, and made it clear that he would enforce his demand with a challenge if necessary.

Apparently they believed he was bluffing, and, by a determination among themselves, Ward was the one to call the bluff. This consisted of nothing more than making a speech to about a dozen assembled youths along the lines Karl had specifically forbidden. Edith and Giles looked on and studied Karl's reaction. He told Ward to stop, advised the assembled youths to go away if they really liked Ward and wanted to help him.

It was Ward's big test. He met it by an eloquent condemnation of Karl and all who were "afraid of the truth," then resolutely continued. Karl left and Ward's speech took on a triumphant new eloquence. But before it was over one of the boys who had been listening, and had left to follow Karl, returned with the news that Karl had posted a challenge of Ward.

During the three day waiting period Ward made some efforts to argue the injustice of the thing with anyone he could get to listen but Edith and Giles were silent and remained at home.

The combat took place as scheduled. In less than three hours after entrance into the combat area, Karl carried out Ward's body and laid it at the entrance gate before the assembled crowd of those waiting. The dead man was covered with blood, and Karl had taken a superficial stab in his left arm which was blood covered from the shoulder down. The spectacle he made as he laid the man he had killed down and turned to walk away was impressive. The crowd was awed and silent.

Giles couldn't pass up the occasion. He launched into a denoucement of the "murderer." He soared to eloquent heights in which he implicated the seven directors as routinely conspiring with "murderers." He appealed for "justice." Karl, sobered and exhausted by the experience he had been through, stopped and listened a few minutes. Then without a word he went to the assembly house and posted a challenge against Giles.

Four days later a similar drama was enacted but without oratory or blood. Karl again carried his opponent from the field of combat after they had been in overnight. Only a red line around Giles throat told that Karl had in some way used the cord to kill his opponent.

Edith looked on in silence. Margaret came up to Karl and without speaking or touching him walked away by his side.

I suppose what happened to Edith before the summer was

172

over was inevitable in the combination of her nature and the circumstances. Karl forbade her to attempt to leave, as she, of course, would have to realize he would. She took on a new role of a sad, mystical and lonely woman conspicuously working on her garden plot with a spectacular East Indian shawl draped around herself. She made the most of the way the role gave character to her plain face. She also made the most of emphasizing her womanliness. Her body was fairly good. Soon she attracted some sympathy and kind attentions from two adolescent boys. Before long a gathering of several boys was gravitating to her house. There seemed to be the beginning of a matriarchal household presided over by a sad-eyed woman reverting to her trancelike manner. She apparently was avoiding for the moment the line of agitation that Karl had specifically forbidden the three to take, but he watched her activities closely and made a point of getting acquainted with the boys who frequented her place.

Her game of building up her power over the boys by fear of rape accusations was obvious. If she had studied the trials here she would have realized that the game not only had precedents; the solution also had precedents. Usually it has been the father or older brother that saved an enmeshed adolescent boy who could not sort out his own developing emotions cleanly enough to challenge the woman himself. But Karl felt his obligation. He challenged and killed her.

Karl had been in active military combat and probably the thought of taking human life had lost some of its usual emotional impact for him. There is nothing to indicate that his killing those three persons had a strong emotional effect on his life.

The memory of his love for Kirk's mother and his helplessness as he watched the landslide cover her continued to dominate his being. For several years after bringing the four here and killing three of them, he spent much of his time writing. It was during this time that he wrote and first produced the operas. For about three years he lived with Margaret and she bore him a child who died when about six months old. The child was a girl. There is some suggestion that he may have emotionally associated it with Kirk's mother. At least when it died his depression apparently equaled that which he went through when Kirk's mother died.

Some people think Karl killed himself deliberately. Some think he went crazy and killed himself without knowing what he was doing — that he was reliving Jan's death and imagined he was removing rocks from her body until he caused a slide. And some

173

think his death was entirely an accident, and it was only by freakish coincidence that the circumstances were identical with that other death. Anyway he went out one night alone and, in the spot where the landslide covered Kirk's mother, the rocks moved again and another landslide killed him. It was a clear, cold night, there was a slight freeze and the weather would not have been expected to start a slide. No one knows why he was in that place at that time.

30.

The last autumn leaves have gone and before the first sign of spring I will have a baby. I feel the wonder and growth of the earth in me, the expansive simplicity of the forest and meadow, and the awesome mystery of a single blade of grass. Yesterday it was warm, the sun came through bare limbs and dried out the leaves underfoot so that they crackled when I walked through them. I went out in the woods alone and sat in a big pile of dry leaves half covered by them with my back against a fallen log and the sun full in my face. The warmth poured into my body and I stored it up, made it part of me, for the days when it will not be there. I watched a blue grouse doing the same thing; we sat and watched each other for a long time. I was lazier; she finally flew away and I kept on sitting. There were some lazy squirrels too. They were out hunting for the last filberts but I saw two stop and spread themselves out on a stump and do nothing but soak up sunshine.

31.

Finally Margaret decided to open up to me. She certainly picks her own time for such things. I've been trying to make friends with her since the first time I met her and getting nowhere. Always I have felt that she liked me as I do her; but she has always — with an unmistakably affectionate smile but with unmistakable deliberation — closed me out.

I suppose some of her behavior pattern comes from her relations with men. Apparently men find her very attractive. She seems to be so sure of that attraction that there's nothing of the flirt in her. Still there's no touch of conceit, not even any hint of overconfidence in her manner. She just seems to love life so deeply that she never questions but what anyone — man, woman, child, or animal

174

— will love her in return if singled out for the focus of her attention. She's something very fine but very natural and earthy.

She played Erda in the opera and the character was made just by casting her. When Erda first came on and answered Wotan's demand to know who she was, her words were the being of Margaret: "My father called me a child of the earth but the name is not important. You only need know that I am a woman and, of what is significant, all things that were I know, all things that are, and all things that ever shall be." Those words were written by Karl, Kirk's father, for whom Margaret bore a daughter, a daughter who died as a small baby. I have no doubt that Margaret was Erda in his mind when he wrote them. She has three living children by three different fathers, no one of which is Dag, with whom she now lives. I have no reason to ask and no one has volunteered any information but there have probably been more men than these five who have known what it is to have her attention focus on them.

She came to see me on a stormy afternoon when Kirk was away on an overnight trip with Dag and she knew I would be alone. I saw her coming down the road through the woods just before the rains were ready to break. The wind and clouds that were bringing the rains were filling the entire world with fast moving gray, lead-colored and purple tattered forms. The winds raced through the tree tops and over the meadow clearing away all small obstacles, and the clouds came across the windswept earth like heralds bearing the storm's colors. They proclaimed that the storm was on its way.

Margaret seemed on intimate terms with the weather. She had a package in her arms and her coat pulled tight around her graceful form but she was bareheaded, her brown hair blowing in the wind. The joy in her face as she looked at the roughness of the clouds and responded to the forceful sensuousness of the wind made the wild idea pass through my mind that she could have a child fathered by that storm.

Even after she was in by the fire she continued to look out the window when the wind came in strong gusts and the rain rattled against the house, as if her mind were still out there. Her eyes lighted like they might have done if the storm had been an impatient lover seeking her attention.

I love stormy weather and I listened to the same sounds and looked to the window, feeling the same mood that I could see in her, but I felt that any remarks about the weather between us

175

would be indiscreet. I said nothing. Her relationship to the storm was too intimate to be discussed. I felt that in relation to it she would consider us to be rivals.

However I was to learn that, in her thoughts, anyone capable of being her rival meant a woman who was woman enough to be her admired companion. I was to learn a lot about her that afternoon.

Margaret is in her mid-thirties; as age goes she's almost old enough to be my mother; but she looks young, ageless, and I have always felt that it was as one woman looking at another that she looked at me. When she first came in I might have believed that my conspicuous pregnancy weighed in her long-delayed decision to now be friendly with me. For the moment she could see me as the more matronly figure and she the more slim and attractive to men. But she quickly acknowledged my pregnancy as an understood and joyful experience known only to women, but not the whole of our beings.

"You look big and cumbersome and pleased with your burden," she said almost as soon as she was within the door, "Welcome to the clan."

I took her coat but she found a place and set the package down herself. "I'll show you what I've brought you after you have given me some tea and brandy," she said. "Better have something in your tea yourself if you think the baby can take it. This is a picture I brought you and it may be a shock to you."

Her tone was light enough not to disturb me with the seriousness of what I was to see but I had a little brandy in my tea anyway. I brought a jug in by the fire with the teapot and she drank two or three cups with just enough tea to warm the brandy and make it fragrant.

After we had settled down fully and the storm had quieted to no more than a blowing rain, she said, "I know you have thought we had some confidences to get off our chests because we both came from the outside and even both from the same school but, as far as I'm concerned, there isn't anything relevant connected with our background. I have been here seventeen years. This is now the world to me. I'm no longer interested in the other except for the danger it poses for us. My interest in you is tied up with this picture."

It was a big painting but it hadn't seemed over bulky when she was carrying it in the wind. It was carefully wrapped in paper and cloth. She found a good light by a window, unwrapped it and set it up for me to see — then stepped back and watched me. She wanted to see my first reaction.

I know what it was she saw in my face — incredulous surprise. At first glance I thought it was a picture of me. I couldn't imagine who could have painted it. But the idea passed in a moment. The features and coloring were close to mine and the woman in the picture was about my age — but even on canvas she was more alive than I. I'd never even dreamed of being such a person and I knew that in reality I was much less than my dreams.

Margaret watched my face and, as if reading my thoughts, she said, "No, she really isn't you, is she?" At the moment I read a note of relief into her voice; later I decided it was disappointment.

"Who is she?" I asked. I could still hardly believe what I saw.

"Jan. Kirk's mother." Then after a moment she added, "My rival."

She poured herself another drink and sat down with it where she could see the picture. I, too, sat down where I could study it with further care. I had another cup of tea. The painting was signed by Karl.

"You know she was killed in a landslide four years before I came here," Margaret said. "I never saw her but that is the only woman of whom I have ever been envious. I transferred some of that feeling to you when I first met you. You and I both can now be envious of her together. She is a god who once walked this earth. As of now, we, still, are all too human."

I felt a world sliding out from under me. "I had no idea," I told her, "that Kirk was in love with a mother-image and for him I was just a symbol."

"Oh, come out of it," Margaret said. She touched my hand just a moment but held the touch until I was fully conscious of it. When I had come back to reality she added understandingly. "I haven't thought of such an oversimplified idea pattern in seventeen years."

After I had given it a second thought, I admitted without reservation that my reaction had been silly. Kirk was only four when his mother was killed. I asked why she wanted to give me the picture.

"I have to do something with it," she said. "She's already immortalized as Brunnhilde in the opera. I can't burn it — I'm not that sacrilegious; but if the picture falls into the hands of romantic men they'll build a shrine for her."

I pondered her meaning a moment and understood, but I protested, "Not the men here."

"I'm afraid so," she insisted. "This is a stronghold against men's over-romanticism but don't let that fool you. Even our men's love of ideals would run off into sterile dreams if we let them start setting up an ideal woman." After a moment she added, "If there's a woman more ideal than you or me or any woman here, no man should spend time looking at her unless the ideal can be seen as living flesh and blood and bone." I knew that painting captured the soul of a real flesh and blood woman. She *had been* living but now she was only a picture.

Margaret paused. I could see she had something that she considered important to say so I waited.

"I have lived with her," she nodded toward the picture, "half a lifetime. I'm going to walk away and leave her sitting there and you can put her in the fireplace, show her to your children as their grandmother, or do with her what you like. But I think you are woman enough not to burn candles before her."

I looked again at the picture and imagined myself kneeling before it with an upturned face reverent in candlelight. Searching for the disdain I expected, I didn't find it. The expression on the woman in the picture didn't change. Almost I could hear her silence say to the worshipful upturned face, "I don't relate to you." But because I wanted to try to relate to her, I suddenly knew I could hang her in my room and live with her.

Glancing at Margaret I caught the expression on her face and knew she also could and had lived with the picture half a lifetime — perhaps as her only real woman companion. She poured herself another full cup of brandy and didn't put any tea in it.

She stayed all afternoon and drank an awful lot. I marvelled at how little the brandy seemed to affect her and decided it was because her conscious and unconscious being are all of one piece. I think her visit may have had more than one purpose and I think she did her part in getting everything across. But I'm not sure I got it all.

Her bringing the picture to me was somehow related to the fact that she had been chosen as one of the Hundred. However both the picture and becoming one of the Hundred were only outward signs of something that was happening within her and it was this that she wanted to tell me, or, in some way, show me. I think it's oversimplifying to say that what she wanted to show me was her intellectual yes-saying to what it means to be a woman, but I think that was one aspect.

Those of the Hundred stand between Camp 38 and the outside world, so they have to look analytically at our differences with a view to preserving them. They have to consider everything as generals looking at military strategy. They plan the strategy of our relations with the outside world, and they set deliberate precedents for day to day living here. After being chosen, Margaret was now thinking analytically about what it means to be a woman.

All those of the Hundred are strongly involved with the future. They are also involved in curtailing certain patterns from the past that have been unthinkingly preserved. Here, two opposing tendencies — the tendency to love existing reality and preserve the past, and the tendency to love the future enough to destroy part of the present — are seen as innate sexual characteristics that distinguish woman and man. This idea featured prominently in the part of Margaret's thought pattern that she showed me that day.

She began by saying, "You know how I came here, so I won't go into that, but I want you to know that I think Karl was right in killing off three of us after bringing us here. He would have been entirely justified if he had killed me too. Although I didn't try to upset the life here, I had too much zombi conditioning to be a real woman. She," indicating the picture with a nod of her head, "was woman enough to keep Karl in contact with the world as it is. I managed to do it for a while but, in the end, I lost him to a dream of the future."

Identification of woman with the past and man with the future is so common here that she apparently assumed that would cause me no trouble. However she seemed to think it necessary to add her own views to the concept, generally accepted here, that it is desirable to further accent male-female differences. She talked of the desirability of pressing innate differences to the greatest extreme of tension that a man and woman can bear, so as to intensify their sexual beings. She said that both gain stature if, in each movement of the two together into their separate worlds — worlds that can never mesh — they deliberately carry the pendulum to a greater extreme. She said that, in doing so, each becomes alternately less utterly man and less utterly woman. Then, when the pendulum moves back, each becomes more intensely one's own sex, and can give the pendulum still another push to further increase sex-differences. She was clearly advocating a conscious effort to increase differences between men and women, even though she saw the differences as being already very great. Everything she said recognized the existent differences.

179

In talking about her relations with Karl, she said, "A woman has to make a deliberate effort to think of a future beyond her children, but a man does it instinctively. A man sees the present with his eyes; his thoughts are constantly in the future — and his hands reach for it. A woman's hands feel for the present; she feels the future in her guts. By instinct she doesn't reach for the future until her fingers can touch it and her arms hold it."

Something was evolving in her being that was related to the Hundred and related to me. It joined her, me, and the Hundred because we are all consciously concerned with the purpose of Camp 38. It also related her to me because her life had been entangled with that of Kirk's father and vicariously with that of his mother. But mostly I think it related her to me because we could see each other as women, and what was happening to her was happening to her as a woman. She wanted me to see it. She wanted me to see it in her. And she wanted me to see it in the picture she brought me.

Margaret is logical but the emotional aspect of things is their major reality for her. As she tried to say things that can't be said in words her attempts and, perhaps also her meanings, often found expression in her face and body attitudes. It has long been recognized that a man is known by what he does; a woman by what she is. Margaret is a woman. I imagined how much a man could come to love being with her, listening to her low voice, and watching her.

"A woman *feels* the present," she said, and as she said it she seemed to be feeling everything for a moment intensely with her fingers, with her face, with her body, seeing it with her eyes, breathing it into her being and relishing its taste to show me what she meant. "A woman can *think* of the future rationally by a conscious effort if she is moving into the thought pattern with a man she loves. But for a woman the future, as an intellectually conceived ideal, is something that's pretty unreal. It's different with a man. Ideal worlds of the distant future are instinctively grasped for by men. And when men lose empathy with women they remain in those other worlds so completely that the future worlds become their heaven or hell."

After a moment, when she seemed to be remembering something, she went on: "Living with Karl taught me the kind of unreal heaven or hell a man can get lost in. I can probably best explain to you what I'm talking about by referring to the outside world. In the outside, people rant against wars fought for inane purposes. But the outside world is held together by fighting those inane wars.

180

More than that, it is held together by glorifying the sterile abortions of men's dreams as something worth fighting for. It dignifies those man-made abortions by calling them science, logic, or creative art. Some of the results may have a temporary value but they come about like a pearl made by putting an irritant in a shell with an oyster. I have seen it in Karl and I know that what produces art is lonely suffering. If a man is to have any joy in being, he has to remain in contact with the present, and that contact is sufficient only when his present holds a woman he can see, touch, and be glad that the path to his future is within her."

The simplest part of what she was saying about a man, who instinctively feels for the future with his hands, was that, if he reaches for the future and only grasps thin air, he will turn and crush a portion of the present to get something plastic that he can mold. "A woman needs to know this by intimate knowledge of some real man," she said. "That is the only way a woman can accept it. A woman doesn't *feel* that way; a woman wants to preserve what is. She cherishes the past. Often she even wants to preserve, or return to, the aboriginal oneness. That past oneness is a highly cherished part of her being. Except as an extension of the present the future doesn't exist for her. There are times when a woman is horrified by what she sees a man do, and must accept as something motivated by a morality utterly foreign to the morality that is born in her being. To accent and add value to her own being she must accept the *acts* of a man — acts of that portion of the aboriginal oneness that evolved into multiple creative beings who love the future enough to destroy some of the present."

I told her that I do accept it. It is something I have learned to accept since I have been here.

She wanted to be sure I was looking at the same thing she was, so she gave me some examples. Even though I was brought up in contempt of over-tender religions, I became so disturbed by some of the things she offered as examples to be accepted with full understanding that I burst out, "Consciously planning the future and destroying the present in *that* way is aspiring to become a god."

She smiled with a little twist in the corner of her mouth at her unstated opinion of what I was saying. She looked in the fire a long time. Then she answered me indirectly by commenting quietly: "Do you know that she," pointing at the picture with a lift of her chin, "wouldn't be able to understand your using the word "god" in that way? That's the big difference between us and her. You make that comment and I understand you. She was born a god.

181

She lived as a god — a real god, a decisive creator of her own being as a woman. She lived as a god without thinking about it. She looked about her for other gods, in the hope of finding comrades — not beings to worship or from whom to learn values.

She paused, looked at the picture a long time, looked at me briefly, then went on:

"We are of the same blood and bone, but you and I still bear the cultural taint of a religion created by slaves — slaves who looked to something outside themselves for the authority to be themselves. We think we have to approach being what we are with humility, trembling before absent masters whose roles we suspect we may be usurping."

It was only a slip into an old habit of thinking on my part and we didn't get sidetracked into discussing something on which we both consciously agree. I regreted the slip. I resolved to keep quiet and let her talk after that. I wanted to relate to her. I wanted to absorb what she thought a woman must be if man's and woman's separate worlds are to become greater — if they are to have a more ecstatic tension between them, not merge and flatten each other out.

I wanted to relate to her. But after her last comment she looked in the fire and turned her cup around in her hands a long time. For awhile I was afraid she might suddenly jump up, take the picture back under her arm and leave. I was inordinately happy to hear in her tone that she wasn't going to do that. Her tone told me that before I had heard enough for the words to have meaning. But I think the words themselves said something too. As nearly as I can remember, she said:

"You and I came from a part of that outside world where the old group-gods had been traded for a new fad in group-gods called governments. But the old pre-history thought pattern remained unchanged. Whether we called it god or government, we still accepted something outside ourselves as having some occult prerogative to overrule our own volition. We are now trying to escape our zombi conditioning and accept the manifest reality that the aboriginal intelligence has evolved into multiple beings of two sexes. Although each sex embodies the other sex in recessive form, one can fully know the other only by intimate acquaintance.

"As women, we look with awe on strong men who show respect for their mortal opponents by formalizing a fair fight to the death. When we broaden the perspective of conscious individual sovereignty to include women, we see that the relationship between women becomes something utterly different from anything in the outside world. Here no hypothesized god, government, or society has created and set up a fictional role-model for a woman to follow. We have no criteria that forces us to compete with each other for social approval. One woman looks at another woman as someone against whom she can measure herself woman to woman. There is no synthesized ideal to stand between reality and reality.

"Men recognize that they add strength and stature to their enemies by formalizing combat. Strong men *choose* to do so. Women here seek to give to each other so as to enhance the value of the reality against which they measure themselves. That replacement of all abstract criteria with respect for flesh and blood enemies and rivals gives some hint of the difference between here and the outside. But the whole reality is bigger.

The total difference between here and the outside zombi world is known by tuning ourselves to the billion year old melody of total reality, as that *reality* comes from the past, continues into the present, and can be joyfully anticipated as a projection into the future. Entering a man's world and knowing a man's future-oriented thoughts helps a woman to hear the whole melody. A man's will to destruction comes neither from love of life nor love of death but from love of life's melody, whose *notes* are birth and death.

"When a woman has been into a man's world, she learns from a man the meaning of honor in dealing with an opponent who may become a mortal enemy. In my woman's language, a man's honor is a love for life's melody that is greater than his personal interests. It is the selective actions of a god who feels the creation-old melody in one's god-being — and will not put in a discordant note. Honor, in relation to a mortal enemy, is a deep non-verbal knowledge a man here has because he is born a man. A woman can learn the honor that guides a man's creative destruction from intimate knowledge of a man.

"And it is only by intimate knowledge of a woman that a man learns from woman the meaning of love for those she cherishes.

"I wonder if you have noticed that men here use the phrase 'a woman's love.' A man here may often be even more considerate and tender than a woman, but he recognizes that his actions stem from an impulse different from the deepest impulse of a woman. Here, men are fully aware that 'a woman's love' is something they can know only objectively."

She was silent and immobile for a long time gazing at the fire. She appeared to be collecting her thoughts. As I now remember, I believe she was really just giving me time to think about what she had said. She knew that the commonplace here is something foreign and unknown to the world outside. I *needed* the time she gave to consider what she had just said. I thought about Kirk's use of that phrase, I thought about Kirk's behavior and I thought about some things about it that had puzzled me. She knew I would need years to really think about what she had just said and, after giving me time to realize that, she finally went on.

"As women who have had our ability to think perverted by our years of conditioning outside, you and I face the task of consciously reclaiming — making part of ourselves as individuals — the portion of woman-nature that was taken from us in the history-old process of unsexing us. The part of woman-nature that was taken from woman was assigned by verbal connotations to governments, gods, or any of the various group-uniting phantoms. We don't need to rehash all the method's of doing that, but we need to realize that it left women almost as totally unsexed as the similar process of taking man's individual sovereignty, and giving a hypothesized sovereignty to a group-entity, unsexed men.

"Outside you have seen all the groups of psychotic people frantically reaching with eager fingers and grasping hands for some phantom god of love. The spectacle is pathetic. What those grasping hands are seeking can't come from an abstract god. It can't come from any man-made institution. It can't come from any group of do-good women. It can come only to each individual, on a one-to-one basis, from an individual flesh and blood woman who, in the act of giving, remains whole and individual."

She gave me a little time to think, before saying, "The phrase 'a woman's love' may point to the most graspable difference that you and I can see between here and the outside. It contrasts to the outside phrase, 'God is love.' Here we accept the manifest evidence that the aboriginal creative intelligence has evolved into woman and man — into the will to preserve extant being and the will to create a greater future. The aboriginal creative intelligence has become multiple. The *aboriginal creative intelligence* is not love. Love is not god. It is not the whole essence of the aboriginal creative intelligence.

But the word 'love' does come close to identifying the quality that distinguishes woman from man. Only a woman — an individual woman acting as an individual — can give anything remotely satisfying into those grasping hands.

"But one woman can't give to all that reach for 'a woman's

love.' She can only give of herself and the world that bears her touch to a selected few. She needs to select them with the unequivocal decisiveness of a real flesh and blood god."

She didn't look at me. She didn't try to *show* me the full impact of her words. I understood and appreciated her restraint. She turned her cup slowly around in her fingers while her being seemed to fill again like a well from an underground spring. Then she went on.

"Life has taken half the time since the aboriginal creator became a biological entity to evolve a man and a woman who are conscious of their god heritage. That *conscious* knowledge makes for a very precarious balance. However, the capability of living as a god with that conscious knowledge already exists. The god-perspective comes from listening to the total melody that makes life a continuous joy. It comes from recognition that the joy of relating to others, whose individual deep-rooted impulses cause them to add to or oppose one another's efforts, is a shared appreciation of life's whole creation-long melody. It comes from seeing one's very blood and being becoming the notes of life's melody, and one's creative volition a part of the whole continuing creation. For you and me, who came from the zombi world, it means the new understanding that living is not a game played for a prize; it is seeing, feeling, listening to, and participating in the point-counterpoint complexity of life's full orchestration."

Margaret has wonderfully happy relations with her children, and the portion of time she gives to them won't be reduced by her activities as one of the Hundred. Also she's in the full flower of her appeal to men as a woman and has no intention of squandering her potential. But I feel that she was trying to tell me of something beyond what she already is.

It was not the theory of the whole scheme of sexual division; it was the pictured reality of woman's part in the stepped up intensity of being that she was trying to set before me. She didn't want me to become smug in my biological fulfillment. She wanted me to see a further stage beyond simple maturity — a stage of being that I might someday move into with confidence. It would mean throwing out the last of my zombi ideas, and that would shake me with a terrible fundamental destruction. But in the end I would experience a rapturous renaissance.

I think I glimpsed it. But I can't write it down because I only *glimpsed* it and didn't *live* it. What I saw in Margaret was the process of metamorphosis. The picture she brought me was of a being bred and born by the aboriginal-oneness-become-multiple into a god-woman.

I know the picture of Jan hanging in my room is going to become very important to me. But I think much of its meaning for me will come from the memory of Margaret sitting by the fire turning her cup around sensually in her hands, looking at the portrait she was leaving with me, and trying to make me feel what she felt about being a woman. Her attitude and the things she told me tied together; she wanted to know me as a real live woman in lieu of the picture she was giving up. The picture I have of her as I saw her through the window coming up the road in the approaching storm will also stay with me. Almost the same mood picture was repeated when she left.

She got up, slipped quickly into her coat and showed that she wanted to leave without having me show her out. I stood up but said nothing. In letting herself out she turned to me with the same smile she had given me on other occasions. "If you cherish my rival," she looked at the picture as if giving me a dare, "I may come to cherish you."

I tried to smile back in kind. How successful I was I can't know but the newly understood meaning of her smile — the same smile she had always given me — will be something I'll hold in my being and hope that it will someday well up as an integrated part of myself.

I watched her caught up in the storm again. She turned her face up to meet a gust of rain whipped into a solid sheet of force by the wind, and laughed at its force with her mouth half open. I know she was tasting it on her tongue.

32.

I've started my new book of things that can be put into those words whose meanings are clear enough to pass on to my children. Kirk, Boleen, and Wang are letting me use their books so I can compare them for differences that will make me think for myself. It will take a lot of time and thought if I'm going to sift my knowledge enough to avoid making my children's minds into encyclopedias of trivia. I'll probably not be writing here any more.

I feel that this is a sort of cocoon I'm leaving behind me. . . . Cocoon? At first I said scream. Still the same thought — an evidence of birth, reincarnation, metamorphosis.

I don't know which word is more accurate, but I think whatever impulse prompted my writing has been served. I now look back on this battle with my zombi training as something that's no longer a part of me. I feel that what I have to say to myself and other adults may soon be beyond the scope of words. Already a joy that can be articulated by no less than my whole being cries out that I'm becoming a woman.

AFTERWORD

Putting my name as author on this book is far from accurate. The original draft was completely written by John Harland. Since then numerous others have added to the ideas it originally contained, and have even written the actual words of some passages that are part of the finished work.

I merely injected two of my fantasies as my major contribution to the whole:

1. I fantasized myself as being brought from the zombi world into the one here after it had reached the state of development that John had imaginatively described.

2. I fantasized that I was not really I; that I was what I might have been if I had followed the pattern expected of me by my family and friends and gone to the University of California at Berkeley.

I think that it is only because I took so long (over five years) to rearrange the already written book to fit my fantasies that John and everyone else began to call it my book; and, finally, everyone insisted that it should be published under my name. I let myself be persuaded. Because of the emotional attachment I developed for it during those years, I feel that it really is mine, even though only by adoption.

Jill von Konen

189

Significant Books

published by

SOVEREIGN PRESS

"Dedicated to Individual Sovereignty"

The word "Sovereign" in our firm name

was chosen because it ties to our masthead motto

and gives meaning to our purpose as a publisher.

We proudly present

a representative sampling of our publications.

These can be ordered direct from publisher.
Publisher pays postage
(including foreign) when payment is included with order.

Take 40 percent discount on 10 or more copies same title.

SOVEREIGN PRESS, 326 Harris Rd., Rochester, WA 98579

70014 THE ANCIENT STORY OF SELENTAG. A mythological account of decorated trees, mysteriously appearing presents, and the twelve days of the winter solstice celebration. Written to make children happy and scholars thoughtful. This is the little booklet that was so much in demand when listed in W.H. Wilson's VERTICAL FILE INDEX, January 1977 under: "Myths—SANTA CLAUS". Paperback, saddle-stitched, 5x6¾, 46 pages. Printed in brown ink on high quality tan book paper. A holiday gift book. $1.00

5½x8½ paperback

permanent quality

$5.00

84170 BRAVE NEW WORLD, A Different Projection. John Harland.

A rebel of the sixties generation has now matured and found words for his thoughts. In San Francisco John Harland, at nineteen, and an eighteen year old runaway named Jill, joined forces to create a new world.

Along with his examination of various lifestyles he and Jill explored, he examines what's wrong with the establishment, with emphasis on manipulation by word-conditioning, and looks at many well-known doomsday books, such as Huxley's *Brave New World,* Orwell's *Nineteen Eighty-four,* and Zamyatin's *We.* Harland may not be voicing the consensus thoughts of the sixties rebels but his world is startlingly new — and exclusively for the brave. Suitable for classroom discussion.

Permanent quality 5½ × 8½ paperback 144 pages $5.00

BRAVE NEW WORLD, A Different Projection by John Harland recommended for library purchase by BOOKLIST. See full review in BOOKLIST 9-15-78.

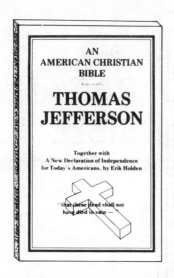

AN
AMERICAN CHRISTIAN
BIBLE

THOMAS
JEFFERSON

Together with
A New Declaration of Independence
for Today's Americans, by Erik Holden

"that these Dead shall not
have died in vain —"

$5.00
paper
128 pages

82146 AMERICAN CHRISTIAN BIBLE, extracted by Thomas Jefferson. Jefferson's extracts from the Bible were not made public until 1902 and are still suppressed. The reason for this is important to every American, and especially to those of Northern European heritage.

The God called "Father" by Jesus was a God of individuals; this made the teachings of Jesus fully compatible with the aboriginal religion of the Northern Europeans. History has been distorted to cover up this fact. The religion of the Jews, who violently condemned Jesus for blaspheming against their *groupism* religion, was imposed upon, identified with, and used to mutilate the teachings of Jesus.

Thomas Jefferson, who carefully worded reference to a creator in the Declaration of Independence "Nature and Nature's God," considered himself a *real* Christian — but felt that he had to keep private his own version of the Bible; he had used scissors to cut away from the words and story of Jesus the mutilating Judaic injections.

This book contains a reproduced photocopy of Jefferson's work, along with an up-to-the-minute examination by Erik Holden of Christianity, biological development, and the all important relationship between religion, state, and individual sovereignty.
Permanent quality 8¼ x 5¼ paperback $5.00

THE PAGAN BIBLE

$5.00
hardcover
296 pages

62012 THE PAGAN BIBLE. Melvin Gorham. "Pagan" originally designated one who would not conform to the state religion of Rome. Later the word was used to point out — in attempted derision — one who would not conform to any of the currently popular religions around the Mediterranean: Christianity, Judaism, and Mohammedanism.

Accepting the challenge implied in the historical meaning of the word, Gorham examines all major religions of the world from the Pagan perspective. The examination sears more often than it praises but the end result is not a barren waste. From the seeming ruin, the ghost of a Pagan, who has endured generations of cloyingly benevolent group rule, rises up in heroic stature to demand a new incarnation.

This work arranges known realities into a conceptual framework that appeals to one who says "I am," "I perceive," and "I will." It shows that a fully conscious Pagan can find a way of life as far evolved beyond that advocated by the "devoutly confused" followers of institutional religions as the highest man is evolved beyond the most primitive organism of the Paleozoic slime. This is not a book for everyone, but the perceptive reader will arrive at a new plateau where a human individual has fully understandable meaning with relation to the total universe — and the total universe also has clear meaning.   296 pages hardcover $5.00

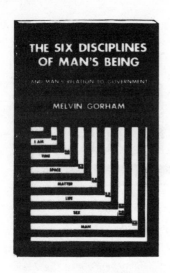

83162   THE SIX DISCIPLINES OF MAN'S BEING and MAN'S RELATION TO GOVERNMENT.   Melvin Gorham.

Gorham examines the life-direction pointed by evolutionary development and inherited memory with special attention to the meaning of sex. He carefully defines (1) Time (2) Space (3) Matter (4) Life (5) Sex (6) Man, and posits "an ultimate frame of reference" for total reality.

After looking with new eyes at reality unincumbered by cultural trimmings, he considers governments.   Most governments are seen as surrogate parents that promote the anti-nature culture of mass manipulation.   The history-old continuity of the oppressive practice suggests hopelessness. Then an opening is revealed which shows that a government can be the implement of all nature, and of nature's man, joined in one action.   This is not a Utopian dream of the future.   It is a clear possibility and there is a plan for immediate action.

Permanent quality, 5¼x8¼ paperback, 128 pages $5.00

Excerpt from a review of **THE SIX DISCIPLINES OF MAN'S BEING and MAN'S RELATION TO GOVERNMENT**

"Melvin Gorham will be read and studied for centuries after today's bestseller authors have been buried with the people who found their books amusing."

— Burton Frye, RFD News, Belleview, Ohio

79111 THE RING CYCLE. Melvin Gorham. This tense adventure story, dealing with violence, political corruption, the meaning of sex, and marriage versus no marriage has appeal for the reader with or without a Wagnerian background. By magnifying a point of contrast, it brings the Garden-of-Eden and the older Babylonian story of two lovers in a garden to the reader's mind for new examination. Brunnhilde's *Gottingarten* is a place entirely separated from the serpent and her Pagan pantheism knows joy as the soul of creation. This clear, powerful portrayal of the spirit permeating the Northern Europeans of prehistory opens the door on a whole new world where intellect and emotions are in full agreement.

79111	Hardcover $8.95
79103 5¼ x 8¼ permanent quality paperback	$5.00

Gorham sets his interpretation of Wagner's Ring operas in the 21st Century "to permit full freedom in translating the subconscious symbols into their present day counterparts." He explains: "The concept of 'nations' might otherwise be an obstacle. The subconscious, of course, can have no symbol for nation other than a living organism — a giant creature, man-like when looked upon as something with which communication is possible, dragon-like when looked upon as a thing to be fought. The mythology of the Northern Europeans was concerned with the undesirable aspects of the nations pressing in upon them from the Mediterranean shores. Nations, per se, were to them essentially undesirable, even as they became to the American Indians. The reverse concept, instilled in every school child in the current world, creates an understandable tendancy *away from* letting the subconscious symbols of the Ring operas come up and find their counterparts in waking consciousness. The viewpoint of the prehistory Northern Europeans is more closely approached here by depicting the 'nations,' not as the institutions known with reverence, but as police-states controlled by gansters with a political facade — as might happen after atomic wars had reduced the metropolitan world to a few cities too minor to have been prime targets."

THE RING CYCLE contains full text of **THE VALKYRIE,** which was originally printed separately, given a full review, and "Recommended for university theater departments" by **LIBRARY JOURNAL.**

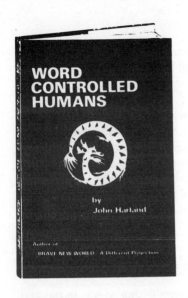

$5.00

paper

128 pages

81138 WORD CONTROLLED HUMANS, A Brief History.
John Harland.   Brief and crystal clear, this would be an
admirable basic work before any other history is studied in
the schools.   The two major conflicting concepts of how life
should be lived are described as cultural directions that came
into conflict before that conflict reached a climax in the
teachings and crucifixion of Jesus.   The Holy Roman Church's
use of a *false* Christianity to promote a theocracy is sharply
portrayed as the destroyer of both the teachings of Jesus and
the Northern European cultural direction.

Then the American attempt to regain our cultural heritage
of individual integrity is examined.   The two hundred year
long losing battle is covered from the perspective of religion,
government, and money.   Expanding to the worldwide scene,
Harland looks at the errors made by the Germans under
Hitler in trying to recover from the destructive effects of
theocracy.   He keeps his eye on what is significant rather than
merely sensational.

This brief history puts the problems of the human species
into a context where effective action to correct them can be
seen as a present possibility.

81138	Hardcover	$9.00
8112X	5¼x8¼ permanent quality paperback	$5.00

84189 VALORIC FIRE and a WORKING PLAN FOR INDIVIDUAL SOVEREIGNTY. From the Valorian Society.

This unusual book first sets forth an imaginary campfire conference of people with varied pasts who are seeking to form a totally new human relationship based on a new morality. As brands from the burning, they readily reject the theocratic pseudo-morality that has already scorched the earth. Approaching every possible discussion with an alerted suspicion of groupism, they probe for some *new* morality that may be manifest by Nature.

A second section clearly states Nature's morality, dismisses *all* laws imposed on individuals by groups as immoral, and proposes agreements between individuals to limit group power. The proposed "new" agreements are found to be the *old* ones that governed the people of Northern Europe before Christianity. This work gives the precise wording of the seven points of agreement that play a big part in John Harland's *Brave New World,* and in Jill von Konen's *Camp 38.* Also it describes how they may be adapted to form functioning agreements for a current survival group, or for a current group wanting a better way of life than the world of maniupulated zombis.

Permanent quality 5½ × 8½ paperback 128 pages $5.00

SOVEREIGN PRESS, 326 Harris Road, Rochester, WA   98579   U.S.A.

83154 THE FORCE UNDERLYING MASS WARFARE. This is the strategy of the Individual Sovereignty Society for dealing with the causes behind the atomic bomb and all mass warfare—and for restoring constitutional Government in the United States. Emphasis is on the unconstitutional power to control the value of U.S. money given to the Federal Reserve Bank, and the unconstitutional power of censorship given to those controlling radio and television broadcast stations. Contains information about objectives, organization, and qualifications for membership in the ISS.

24 page brochure   **$1.00**

82019 ATOMIC WAR AND YOU. A catalog of Sovereign Press books that contains an extensive statement of this unique company's publishing policy. Individual sovereignty is viewed in the context of biology, history and the current threat to individual integrity. A companion brochure to the above.   **$1.00**

7809X CENSORSHIP IN THE U.S. Marguerite Pedersen. Pedersen is the senior editor of a current and continuing book publishing company. She cites specific names, dates, and facts as examples of extremely widespread censorship within the United States. Emphasis is on conditions in the book publishing industry and manipulation of the purchase procedures within tax supported libraries. This work contains an appendix dealing with NEA, National Endowment for the Arts, which shows how this U.S. Government agency is aiding the censorship imposed by an anti-Government conspiracy.

5¼x8¼ permanent quality paperback   **$3.00**

Excerpt from a review of **BRAVE NEW WORLD, A Different Projection** by John Harland:

"As I predicted, the brighter lights of the rebellion of the sixties would only show their color after the hubbub subsided."

—Burton Frye, REGIONAL NEWS, Lake Geneva, Wis.

82146 AMERICAN CHRISTIAN BIBLE, Extracted by Thomas Jefferson. Together with **A New Declaration of Independence for Today's Americans,** Erik Holden. Covers: Christianity versus Judaeo-"Christianity," media manipulation of U.S. Government, controversy over First Amendment, pseudo-science versus creationism in schools, biological and sociological meaning of maleness and femaleness, the direction pointed by Nature and *Nature's* God, and múch more.

82146 Permanent quality 5¼ x 8¼ inches, paperback $5.00

Here is what an eminent historian says about Erik Holden's examination: "The Biblical analysis was ever-so refreshing and absolutely appropriate. The author has reached for the very heights of the ethical truths that await the renaissance of man."

Thomas Marcellus — Director, Institute for Historical Review

- - - - - - - - - - - - - - - - -

ORDER FORM

To: SOVEREIGN PRESS, 326 Harris Rd., Rochester, WA 98579

Please send me the following: I enclose $ _____ __

Quantity	Title	Extension
	Sales tax (Washington residents)	
	Total	

Name _____

Address _____

_____zip _____

ORDER FORM

Publisher pays postage
(including foreign) when payment is included with order.

Take 40 percent discount on 10 or more copies same title.

To:

SOVEREIGN PRESS, 326 Harris Rd., Rochester, WA 98579

Please send me the following: I enclose $ _____

Quantity	Title	Extension
	Sales tax (Washington residents)	
	Total	

Name _____

Address _____

_____zip _____